Beyond Business
Process Reengineering

We dedicate this effort to the
memory of some uncommon people
MJC
HFD
AMF
KMW
and to our families with appreciation
for their love and unselfish support

Beyond Business Process Reengineering

Towards the Holonic Enterprise

PATRICK McHUGH
GIORGIO MERLI
WILLIAM A. WHEELER III

JOHN WILEY & SONS

Chichester · New York · Brisbane · Toronto · Singapore

Other Wiley Editorial Offices

John Wiley & Sons, Inc., 605 Third Avenue,
New York, NY 10158-0012, USA

Jacaranda Wiley Ltd, 33 Park Road, Milton,
Queensland 4064, Australia

John Wiley & Sons (Canada) Ltd, 22 Worcester Road,
Rexdale, Ontario M9W 1L1, Canada

John Wiley & Sons (SEA) Pte Ltd, 37 Jalan Pemimpin #05-04,
Block B, Union Industrial Building, Singapore 2057

Library of Congress Cataloging-in-Publication Data

McHugh, Patrick.
    Beyond business process reengineering : towards the holonic
enterprise / Patrick McHugh, Giorgio Merli, William A. Wheeler III.
        p. cm. ——
    Includes bibliographical references and index.
    ISBN 0-471-95087-4
    1. Industrial management.   2. Strategic alliances (Business)
I. Merli, Giorgio   II. Wheeler, William A.   III. Title.   IV. Title:
Holonic enterprise.
HD31.M38836   1995   94–30745
658.8—dc20   CIP

British Library Cataloguing in Publication Data

A catalogue record for this book is available from the British Library

ISBN 0-471-95087-4

Typeset in 11/13pt Palatino by Dobbie Typesetting Ltd, Tavistock, Devon
Printed and bound in Great Britain by Bookcraft (Bath) Ltd

Contents

Authors' Preface

Approximately two years ago two of us, Patrick McHugh and Bill Wheeler, co-authored a book on business process reengineering (BPR). Frankly, it was not the runaway best seller that our competitor's book was, but we felt satisfied that we had fully articulated the strategic aspects of BPR. We wrote of three types of BPR:

1 The first concentrated in single functions of a business and was predominantly a cost reduction effort.
2 A second type which began to cross functions and was aimed at achieving competitive parity.
3 The majority of the book dwelt upon the third type which we called BreakPoint. The idea was to identify customer or market values such as speed, flexibility, etc. which when realized would result in redefining the market rules to the advantage of the practitioner. We argued that the realization of such excellence could be achieved only when a company "broke the china" and optimized core business processes around those market values.

At one of our recent international meetings we were bemoaning the fact that most companies undertaking BPR were concentrating on Type 1. We wanted to get companies to stretch the reengineering concept to Type 2 or, preferably, Type 3. We briefly discussed writing another book that would become almost a crusade for "breaking the china", but we felt another campaign would only belabor the first. We then set out to discover why companies were sub-optimizing such a powerful tool as BPR.

We made a big mistake in our first book (as have all the others). We concentrated on the four walls surrounding a company. We did not extend the breadth of reengineering to other companies in the value chain and treat them as part of the whole process. This books seeks to rectify our wrong.

We first set out to write a book about the mechanics of extending processes up and downstream (Chapter 5 discusses the details of Co-Makership and Demand Driven Logistics). As we developed outlines and philosophical under-pinnings we began to understand where businesses were unconsciously moving. We came to realize the dynamics of why companies were being forced toward holonics. The escalating cost and speed of innovation and technology, the rise of prosumerism, and the market need for almost instant gratification are all factors that drive us beyond the bounds of conventional BPR.

Dr Robert W. Hall, editor of the Association for Manufacturing Excellence's *Target Magazine*, has written a series of articles describing Total Enterprise Manufacturing (TEM). He writes that TEM is composed of three elements:

1 Virtual which he defines as "teamwork across boundaries of functional departments and/or across established companies"
2 Agile which is the "the ability to rapidly respond; i.e., Turbo JIT"
3 Holonic which is "autonomous distributed systems, whether computer or human systems" (We argue that it is both.)

For our purposes we have chosen to combine the elements under the banner of holonics and have expanded the mechanics of how to create a holonic network and why.

Some of our colleagues were troubled by the title *Beyond BPR*. They were concerned that we would suggest that BPR is no longer appropriate for businesses. Just as TQM and JIT methodologies are necessary for successful BPR, so too is internal or "four wall" BPR a prerequisite for a thriving holonic network. BPR is not dead! It just needs to be stretched to the next level so that companies can more appropriately respond to current and future market forces.

If readers have already consulted their dictionaries as to the definition of holonic, they are probably perplexed (or maybe, peeved) that the word does not appear. Arthur Koestler first created the word "holon" in his book *The Ghost in the Machine* written in 1967. Its derivation is from the Greek "holos" meaning whole and "on" inferring part. Koestler was writing about the operation of systems within systems. For our purposes we have chosen to simplify the concept and write of processes within processes.

The reader may further question why such an international team (USA, UK and Italy) would join together to write a book on holonic business systems. The answer is simple; we all bring a different perspective to a subject which has no formal definitions and scant experienced practitioners. Northern Italy is probably the most advanced in the application of holonic business systems, but its networks tend to be populated with very small companies. (The average Italian company has 45 employees whereas in the US the number is tenfold.) The US, because of its vast geography, has been slower to adopt the concept. It is only now beginning to employ enablers such as information technology and inexpensive air express to advance toward holonic networks. The UK has the geographic proximity, but it has tended to treat nodes more as captive suppliers than as independent nodes. Coming from these different perspectives forced us to work through the concepts in greater depth than we would have had we had only one point of view. One of our pre-agreed "ways of working" was to reach consensus on principles and concepts or they would not be in the text.

Gaining consensus was not always easy. In some cases the Italian, American and British versions of the English tongue got pretty garbled. Patrick McHugh has some understanding of Italian but was totally stumped by the word "plugarun". After repeated queries we finally determined that what was intended was "plug and run" which meant that any node should be quickly available to join a virtual company and at immediate full speed. "Plug and run" stayed in the text.

Many people supported and contributed to our thinking during the development of this book. First, our thanks go to the many clients who took the time to share their thoughts and future strategies with us. These include Michael Davis then of ISS, Ivano Beggio of Aprilia and Heinrich Zimmermann of ABB. Others requested anonymity, but they know who they are. We appreciate their forthrightness and patience with our repeated questions and their time reviewing sections for accuracy. Bob Borsch contributed thoughts on supply line management, Alex Beavers clarified our thinking on process costing, and Ron Barris wrote the section on automation networks. Cesare Saccani of Centro Estero Camere di Commercio Lombarde developed the tourism model and along with Luigi Gambarini took the time to explain it to us. Malcolm Fraser-Urquart and James Warner were invaluable during the development of the demand driven logistics concept. Chris Baker and Andrew Tanswell helped with the British case studies. Mark Stanton and Graham Whitney provided important contributions from their own wealth of experience. Professor Jinichiro Nakane of Waseda University introduced us to Japanese studies on holonic strategies. Oscar Cecchinato and Mariano Roman provided us with the Aprilia data.

Beth Mason of the Wilton Public Library was indefatigable in her quest for statistics and subject matter. Elaine Allen, Meg Carpenter and Daniela Pirovano supported us both in the writing of this book and in our day-to-day activities. Thelma Doyle did the graphics for the book and was the consummate organizer of our diverse activities. To all of these people we say thanks and we appreciate their efforts.

To our wives we owe a special gratitude for putting up with us while we ruined many a family weekend working on the book.

Jon Zonderman had the unenviable task of rewriting all the chapters from our rather stumbling, diverse prose and rambling discussions. Jon was the cohesive force that pulled the book together. His facile grasp of concepts and dogged insistence upon unanimity forced us to rethink our ideas on more than a few occasions. Special and sincere thanks from all of us.

In the Appendix we have listed suggested reading material for the reader wanting to go further into some of the concepts that we have discussed. We should make special note of a few books that were extremely thought provoking and helped us formulate our own ideas. These books include *The Virtual Corporation* by William Davidow and Michael Malone, *The TeamNet Factor* by Jessica Lipnack and Jeffrey Stamps, and *From Value Chains to Value Constellations: Designing Interactive Strategy* by Richard Normann and Rafael Ramìrez. Where possible we have tried to reference them in the text. If we missed any acknowledgements it is not by intent; rather, ideas start to elide after a while.

Special thanks for the support and sharing of information goes to Jessica Lipnack who told us the Erie Bolt story and shared with us her observations of the Emilia-Romagna region.

Just as we did for our previous book, we developed "ways of working" together that served as guidelines for the effort. One of the "ways" was that we were not going to write a consulting book, nor were we going to present a "How To" book. What we have attempted to do is to observe how businesses are managed today, how they are responding to new market demands, and extrapolate from that what will be required in the future. While we cannot claim to have performed extensive academic research, we do believe that the concepts presented are born of the real world and are being further refined as we write.

When one of us told Bob Hall of our intention to write a book on holonic business systems he relayed to us his experience with discussions around holons. "People would immediately roll their eyes back up into their head." He further reminded us of Mark Twain's commentary on business books—"Chloroform in print". We sincerely hope that the reader will keep his eyes focused on the future and at the same time not be anesthetized by the prose. We had fun writing it and we hope the reader will share our enthusiasm.

Waterford, Maine USA
London, England
Milan, Italy
July, 1994

1
The Holonics Concept

Imagine the plight of the MEGA-PC company (a fictional company, but one similar to many existing companies). The company designs, assembles and markets work stations and client servers. The company started in the early 1980s. It then did almost all the tasks associated with designing both its products and the printed circuit boards (PCBs) that went into them. Its plant inserted components into PCBs and in turn assembled the PCBs into the computers.

This was possible then because each new generation of hardware had a lifespan of about two years before it was supplanted by the next. The company thought that performing all these steps in-house would keep costs down. The components were supplied by semiconductor manufacturers, known as integrated merchants. These manufacturers produce integrated circuits (ICs) for sale in parallel with the production of their own downstream electronic systems and subsystems products.

The biggest semiconductor firms hesitated to go it alone on large projects. Besides licensing and trading agreements several joint ventures linked US firms such as IBM, Motorola, Intel and Texas Instruments with their major domestic and foreign competitors.

The market hunger for new products became such that by early 1993, the average personal computer product lifespan was 9.4 months. Worse yet, selling prices of basic personal computers (PCs) often plummeted more than 40 percent in 12 months. Meanwhile, the market required greater and greater product diversity and even customization. This resulted in smaller and smaller manufacturing lot sizes and drove up manufacturing costs.

Often, PCs sell for application-specific uses. Software enables most specific applications, though some applications require new hardware configurations. For instance, PCs sold to banks for "back-office" applications such as check clearing and stock transaction recording are different to those sold for manufacturing shop floor control. One large US PC manufacturer has 70 different configurations of hardware, all of which reside inside a case that looks roughly the same to the casual observer. This all translated for MEGA PC into smaller lot sizes for components.

During the late 1980s and into the early 1990s, increasing performance characteristics and reducing costs were accomplished through the use of application-specific integrated circuits (ASICs). These reduced the population and complexity of components on PCBs. MEGA-PC designed its own ASICs, at a cost of $1–2 million per new IC. Integrated merchants manufactured ICs under contract to MEGA-PC.

The increased costs and reduced price constantly squeezed margins. By 1994, MEGA-PC executives felt the company could not continue to do as much of the IC and PC design as it had in the past. Its assembly and sales business needed ever more attention. The company would have to focus on its core competencies and technologies if it were to be successful in the future. This in turn meant finding partners to incorporate into the process of providing ICs for its work stations and servers.

MEGA-PC began talking to companies whose core business was in the semiconductor industry. It was looking for a way to form a partnership that would allow MEGA-PC to concentrate on its core competencies. The companies were eager to talk to MEGA-PC because their own businesses were also being buffeted by change.

Industry estimates in 1994 were that the $9 billion ASIC market would grow to $21 billion by 1997. However, the PCB and IC industries were having difficulties of their own. Although there are 750 000 new PCB designs annually, 60 percent of them have production volumes of less than 1000 units. A full 80 percent have production volumes of less than 10 000 units. This makes it very difficult for the companies to amortize the $1–2 million design cost for ASICs they design and then manufacture.

Further, a movement started to make PCBs obsolete by multi chip modules (MCMs). These are sealed devices that contain both standard and application-specific semiconductors, sensors and actuators which are mounted on a single silicon wafer with their own circuitry. ASICs, and more so MCMs, are seen by the industry as enablers of miniaturization. Industry estimates were that the complexity of ASICs would quadruple every two years.

The MEGA-PC executives considered that moving design outside the company might cause a problem. The computer-aided engineering (CAE) and computer-aided design (CAD) software used by external designers might be restrictive in that it may only reflect one company's capabilities. These capabilities may or may not be leading edge. Business software has migrated from being home grown to third-party generic. Similarly, by 1994, third party CAE and CAD design software was available commercially, with more flexibility than company-specific systems. The third party CAE and CAD software producers maintain an engineering data base and provide non-protected design data to ASIC and MCM designers through leasing agreements.

Similarly the power and influence of semiconductor manufacturing equipment and materials suppliers had grown immensely. It was even less feasible for semiconductor manufacturers to buy "off-the-shelf" from "arm's-length" suppliers without sacrificing competitive economic or technical advantage.

In the early 1990s, some companies that had provided both design and manufacturing services dropped their manufacturing. This occurred especially if their manufacturing facilities were in "green" countries. Nippon Electric Corporation (NEC) estimates that there is a 20 percent cost disadvantage for production in a "green" country. By 1994, NEC had left IC manufacture to others and concentrated its efforts on rapid, "state-of-the-art" and "correct-the-first-time" design services.

MEGA-PC faced a difficult problem when it decided to look for partners with whom to create a relationship for design and manufacture of its ASICs. Namely, that the industry was becoming increasingly specialized, with companies defining their core competencies and their core business processes in ever more narrow terms.

Complex alliances among semiconductor merchants, their customers, semiconductor manufacturing equipment suppliers and contract assembly firms were becoming a feature in cluster areas like Silicon Valley. Within a few months, MEGA-PC joined forces with several partners, in what we term a holonic network, for the design and production of ASICs and MCMs.

A holonic network is a set of companies that acts integratedly and organically; it is constantly re-configured to manage each business opportunity a customer presents. Each company in the network provides a different process capability and is called a holon.

Each configuration of process capabilities within the holonic network is called a virtual company. By combining the core competencies of many individual companies within the network, each virtual company is more powerful and flexible than the participating members alone could be. Each company in a virtual company is chosen because of its process excellence.

Foundry relationships have been around in the semiconductor industry for years, usually involving larger manufacturing device suppliers. However, "dedicated" silicon foundries that produce no devices of their own design such as the Taiwan Semiconductor Manufacturing Corporation have now appeared. Independent back-end assembly and test firms have long been a part of the industry, they usually are located offshore.

MEGA-PC, however, involved a new type of firm. It was associated with a large semiconductor manufacturing equipment (SME) supplier, based in the US and distinguished by a core competence in high complexity microelectronics assemblies including MCMs.

MEGA-PC is not the only original equipment manufacturer (OEM) that has joined a holonic network. With the rapid changes in ASIC and MCM technology, most PC manufacturers have also found it advantageous to get into a network. They prefer this to trying to maintain the hardware and human capabilities necessary to design their own ICs.

The creation of a virtual company within the IC holonic network happens in the following fashion.

First, MEGA-PC's marketing people feel the pressure of the market for a new generation or upgrade of PC. After the product specifications have been created, the next step is to visit a design center. These centers in the holonic network are staffed by CAE and CAD specialists. These centers are strategically located throughout the world, wherever there are clusters of electronics companies—in the suburbs of Boston, Stuttgart, Haifa and Tokyo.

The center staff has a meeting with the virtual company team that has been assembled for the specific project. The team consists of a MEGA-PC designer and an electrical engineer from the CAE/CAD company. Also part of the team is a quality and reliability engineer from the company that specializes in test services for ASIC and MCM designs. The final team members are a representative from the silicon foundry and a manufacturing engineer from the high-tech assembler. The silicon foundry makes the silicon wafers on which the application-specific circuitry is etched and from which the ICs are cut. The high-tech assembler has the capability for highly complex assembly of devices such as MCMs.

Team members do not negotiate cost; that has been predetermined by the holonic network's pricing formula, which says that each value adding step is worth a given percentage of the final sale price, whatever the market finally decides that to be.

ASIC design is carried out according to a set of design rules agreed to by all network partners regarding tooling sizes, tolerances and test routines. This makes it possible for any manufacturing company to make any product. This in turn allows for the flexible use of capacity worldwide. If the ASIC is going to reside within an MCM, the team will also have a hand in designing that component.

First the team agrees on design and manufacturability. Then the particulars are loaded into the holonic network's ASIC engineering data base, where any partner can use it. If there is some proprietary code that was developed by a team member, that special code is only available to other members on a royalty or fee basis.

The prefabrication of wafers aims to provide as much standardization as possible while allowing for as much customization as necessary. Prefabricated wafers contain about 80 percent of the standardized code necessary to make the ASIC, allowing for economies of mass production and reducing design time considerably. Using this standard platform, the team finishes the design, and the software automatically checks for any logical or physical flaws.

Jumping ahead in time—not too far, for the design allows for production to begin very quickly—MEGA-PC introduces the new

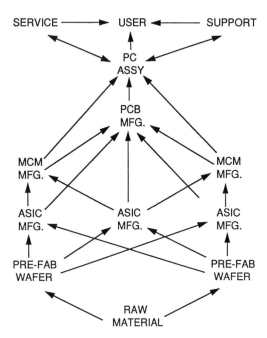

Figure 1.1 *MEGA-PC's holonic network*

model to the market, and it is an instant success. Often such a success causes a production capacity problem. But the usual ramp-up difficulties with a new product with high demand do not occur. This is a feature of working within a holonic network. Here MEGA-PC has reserved capacity with several suppliers. This is because there are several members of the virtual company who have each agreed to devote so much capacity to the effort.

Furthermore the design data base contains standard manufacturing and test instructions. In MEGA-PC, ICs come from two silicon foundries and there are three partners for the assembly of ASICs and two for MCMs. The design and manufacture core business processes of the virtual company are shown in Figure 1.1.

MEGA-PC makes to order. When MEGA-PC receives an order from either a customer or a distribution partner, the PC is assembled, loaded with software and shipped, all within 24 hours.

MEGA-PC sends a daily notification of shipments to the American Express Purchasing Card Division. They "backflush" payment through the entire design-and-manufacture virtual company for the work that went into the production of that one unit.

AMEX uses the bill of material to pay each holon in the virtual company the agreed price of its value add, and any applicable taxes due. Because of this capability, all holons outsource their purchasing and sales tax departments. AMEX also sends a weekly report to an accounting support company that is a separate holon. This in turn prepares the monthly accounting reports for each member of the holonic network. (We will discuss in detail in Chapter 6 the roles of these support holons and the movement toward outsourcing support areas because they are integral in forming holonic networks.)

Deciding which of the manufacturing holons will supply a given IC is a function of the "asset manager" computer program. A "smart chip" that accompanies the lot through the virtual company carries the operating instructions for IC manufacture. It also contains details of the design and pedigree, namely, the previous steps in the value chain. This smart chip not only has operating instructions, but for the sake of payment has the "pedigree" of manufacture. This travelling smart chip also provides lot traceability.

The asset manager in a holonic network has a central role. This means that businesses have come for the first time in a business system to truly depend on advanced computing for their operation. This dependence on a computer system is a result of moving beyond Business Process Reengineering toward a holonic enterprise.

When MEGA-PC sends daily shipment information to AMEX, it also downloads the information into the asset manager. The asset manager polls the available capacity of each holon for each step of the value chain and assesses any core competencies required for special orders. It assigns the work so that it uses the available capacity in the best way and reduces shipping costs and time. South American orders are produced as much as possible in the Western Hemisphere while Asian orders are produced as much as possible in the Eastern Hemisphere. Because semiconductors are so inexpensively air freighted, manufacture in this instance can take place anywhere. This capability gives the asset manager the utmost flexibility regarding

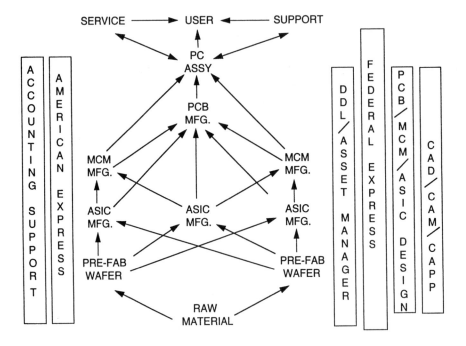

Figure 1.2   *Manufacturing core business process of MEGA-PC surrounded by its support holons*

scheduling worldwide capacity. Obviously, in the manufacture of other large or bulky products transportation is much more of an issue.

The asset manager makes its first pass to reserve capacity. As the specific type of product firms up closer to the actual time of production it reallocates capacity. In this way the asset manager eliminates many forecast errors built into traditional production scheduling programs.

The silicon foundry ships wafers and loaded smart chips by FedEX to the high-tech assembler designated by the asset manager. FedEX acts as the transport holon throughout the virtual company. It handles everything from the raw material to the final shipment of the assembled computers. Because of the fixed routings and captive customers, FedEX is able to reduce significantly the cost of transport below its normal contract rates. Figure 1.2 shows the manufacturing core business process of MEGA-PC surrounded by its support holons.

FedEX is the *de facto* scheduler of the virtual company. It is similar to the system Henry Ford set up, where an empty rail car would be sent from the Ford plant back to the drive shaft manufacturer; this was the signal to finish manufacturing, and then ship another rail car full of drive shafts. There were no orders. The Japanese picked up on this idea and developed it into the kanban system of order replenishment.

The silicon foundries in the holonic network have designed their operations as cells for maximum flexibility and minimum throughput time. Each modular fabrication cell is autonomous and almost fully automated. Each cell contains electronbeam and laser writing equipment, dielectric and metal deposition stations, etching and automated testing machines.

When the silicon dice, or wafers, are received by the high-tech assembler, the smart chip accompanying the dice provides the exact configuration to assemble. A cassette of wafers loaded at the silicon foundry enters the modular assembly cell via an automated material handling device. The first step is to "read" the smart chip on the cassette. Operating and test instructions are loaded into the cell controller, which in turn instructs each piece of equipment. The specific design is found in the engineering data base. Within the cell each wafer is automatically moved from machine to machine on a one-to-one basis wherever possible.

There are no operators in the cells. Engineers in the plant maintain equipment and do sophisticated root cause analysis to further hone the node's core competencies. The engineers also experiment with new technologies for continuous improvement. When they are not in the plant, the engineers meet others in the holonic network. In this way the network builds as much knowledge as possible about the process of making ICs. In this manner, they bring their specific expertise to joint improvement activities for the good of the network.

When the ICs are assembled, the cassette is sent by FedEX to MEGA-PC for use in the final product. The smart chip is updated with required information. The cassette is sent back to the silicon foundry.

From prefab wafer completion to shipment inside a PC the process takes no more than 10 days. The total process cost is an astounding 31 percent less than the old way of doing business.

MEGA-PC, like many of its competitors, has found working within virtual companies and holonic networks to be remarkably invigorating. It now participates in other virtual companies in diverse areas of operations from software development to metal housings. Support areas such as training for PC users and running the company's help lines are now handled by outside companies. In short the PC and server business is now a huge worldwide holonic network of design, manufacture, sales, service and support.

HOW IS YOUR BUSINESS THESE DAYS?

Is your market share flat or falling? Are your margins being squeezed ever thinner? Is there increased competition coming from all directions, including from some unlikely players?

Are customers asking continually for more than you offer—lower prices, better quality, better delivery reliability, faster lead times and more product options? Do you feel that you are falling behind the competition—despite all the improvements your company has made over the previous three to five years?

Is technology outracing you? Is the cost of innovation becoming so great that you are not sure you can keep up? Do you find yourself spending more time on issues about support business processes than you do on improving core business processes?

If the answer to some, or all, of these questions is yes, you are not alone. Most businesses are finding part of the solution is reengineering their organizations to focus the company's efforts on its core business processes. Many are using a framework called Business Process Reengineering that we described in our previous book (Johansson *et al.*, 1993).

Some companies are finding that as they focus more narrowly on their core business processes, they are—like the fictional MEGA-PC—shedding or "outsourcing" some support processes. These support processes include information systems and plant maintenance. The companies are also joining forces with others in holonic networks.

Are you currently involved in any holonic networks with other companies as described above? Would you become so involved?

If you are like many business leaders, the answer is no. And the reason is usually a feeling of control, or more specifically, lack of it. Joint ventures, consortia, and other group arrangements are usually fraught with contractual negotiations, mistrust and distrust. So that, although many companies have tried some form of cooperative arrangements they have been unhappy with the results. Tim Collins and Thomas Doorley (Collins and Doorley, 1991) studied 880 such arrangements. Of these only 45 percent were considered successful by the participants and only 14 percent lasted more than 10 years.

If you are an owner or leader of a small or medium sized independent business—for our purposes defined as between $5 million and $250 million in annual revenues—you are probably reluctant to enter such an effort out of fear of being bullied by larger partners. This is not likely to be the case though as Coopers & Lybrand's "Made in the UK" 1993 survey showed. This focused on "middle-market" companies—defined in the UK as businesses with a turnover of under $300 million. The survey revealed that such companies are normally both suppliers of and customers of other middle-market companies. Similarly, it showed that large companies source mostly from other large companies.

It is just such middle market companies that can make decisions quickly, find opportunity and change corporate direction to capitalize on these opportunities. The economics consulting firm Cognetics, in Cambridge, Massachusetts, calls such companies "gazelles." They pop up and grow rapidly. As *The Economist* reported in its 4 June 1994 issue in an article about California surviving the recession and possibly coming out stronger:

> "After the gold rush, the oil gush and the defense boom, here comes knowledge intensive employment. New businesses are springing up everywhere in telecommunications, entertainment, medical equipment and international trade. The past four years have seen 43 000 corporate relics washed away. In their place have come 33 000 sprightlier firms that have been expanding throughout the recession by a healthy 20 percent or more a year."

Unfortunately for many of you, your reluctance to get involved in joint operations will probably cost you dearly in the next decade. For what is happening throughout the world—driven by companies from Asia to North America to Europe—is a new way of operating jointly, through holonic networks.

Many executives can see the virtue intellectually of joining partnerships of one form or another. However, they are reluctant because they fear "hollowing"—their intellectual property being taken over by a partner—and perceive a loss of control. We believe these fears can be reduced by a successful experience with one or more holonic networks.

But to create such holonic networks, companies must develop a new level of trust. This implies developing a capability to operate without rigidly defined hierarchies and predetermined times. Large and small corporate entities are equal, and no one gets a free ride because of size or reputation. Within a holonic network, any company, large or small, can exploit its core competencies by linking them with complementary core competencies of other companies. This occurs in virtual companies. The virtual company creates the best core business process possible and manages the critical path in real time. But in this network, there must be totally open communications and total trust. Networks that use the holonic business system make it easier for companies to trust each other. This is because each company brings a unique set of core competencies and capabilities to the network. These capabilities and core competencies make them indispensable. Unlike the other types of joint venture arrangements Collins and Doorley point to, holonic networks must be a key operating strategy. Furthermore, participants must consider operating within the holonic network as a "way of doing business." It literally becomes part of their market strategy.

GREATER THAN THE SUM OF ITS PARTS

There are seven characteristics of a successful holonic network. These principles must hold true because if the network closes itself off it will lose its ability to respond to marketplace stimuli. This in turn will cause it to lose its competitive edge.

First, a holonic network is not organized hierarchically. Second, each holon—you can also think of it as a business, a switch within the network or a node, which is our preferred word—has the characteristics of the entire network. In other words, each node is equal to all others. Third, the network is in dynamic equilibrium. Fourth, it is self-regulating. Fifth, access to and exchange of information throughout the network is open, as is access to and exchange of information across the network boundaries. Sixth, the network is evolutionary, and is constantly interacting with its environment. Seventh, it is a knowledge network, and self-learning.

The holonic network is more than just a business association within which virtual companies can form. It is a business system in which information is known to all the participants. Companies respond with their core competencies to the opportunities presented in a real time basis to create a virtual company to respond to any customer requirement. You may think of it as a sophisticated communications switching system, where each communication is automatically routed through the most efficient channels—the particular holonic nodes that present the best core business process—to reach its destination.

The best holonic networks match advanced communication technology with the characteristics of a primitive creature. The Portuguese man-of-war is such a primitive creature, in essence, with a supercomputer for a brain. The man-of-war (*Physalia* is the biological term) is really a conglomeration of creatures, each of which brings a specialization to the whole.

As Art Spikol describes the man-of-war in his murder mystery novel *The Physalia Incident,* it "is really a colony of animals—a variety of creatures called hydrozoans, each group of which handles a particular life function and gradually becomes modified so that it can better handle that function . . . As time goes by, the coordination between the individuals becomes better and better . . . The nervous system becomes ever more integrated as these individuals become more specialized. And the more the individuals become coordinated, the more the colony acts like a single organism."

BPR AND BEYOND

The holonic business system is a natural extension of Business Process Reengineering, and thus goes "beyond BPR." There is a sense in which Business Process Reengineering has become hard wired in individual companies. The core business processes are designed to satisfy in the "one best way" a particular customer need. Many Business Process Reengineering efforts do not seem to consider what will happen if that need changes. The holonic business system allows businesses continually to de-invent and re-invent themselves as they face increasingly ambiguous markets.

Business Process Reengineering experience is now being established. This experience tells us that the leaders of reengineering efforts must turn their attention beyond the analysis of complex process maps and information systems towards two new challenges. First, how can the reengineered core business processes contribute to a strategic repositioning of the business. Second, how to effectively direct and accelerate major organizational change.

BPR focuses on core business processes. It forces each company to define what the five or six processes are that make up the core of its activity. Then Business Process Reengineering makes the company focus on its core business processes, and to think how it can effectively feed resources into these core business processes.

Business Process Reengineering seeks to change the vertical functional pillars of traditional industries into horizontal tubes of process-orientated organizations. Many of today's Business Process Reengineering efforts risk creating as rigid horizontal tubes as the previous vertical ones. In this book, which is concerned with beyond Business Process Reengineering, we recognize that core business processes extend far beyond the boundaries of the single business. Reengineering these cross-company core business processes offers opportunities to serve customers in totally new ways.

There are three kinds of BPR efforts, and these define the scope and ambition of a company's BPR efforts. One is to achieve improvement—usually through cutting cost and aims at support or management processes. It is often accompanied by such efforts as divestment, delayering and downsizing. A second is to achieve "best practice" status in one or more core business processes. Third, some companies seek to achieve a BreakPoint. A BreakPoint is a new level of process innovation—as measured by the value set of cost, quality, lead time, delivery reliability and product functionality—that provides a significant and positive market impact. BreakPoint Business Process Reengineering is concerned therefore to go beyond traditional efforts to improve performance. It has its focus on re-inventing the industry.

The holonic business system extends this idea. For any core business process, a set of nodes within the holonic network can be found that can carry out a core business process in the most effective and efficient manner possible. Essentially, a node can be found that has the core competence to carry out each subprocess within the total core business process. And other nodes can be found that have as their core competence each of the support processes to the core business process.

BPR is market and opportunity driven, and customer focused. So is the holonic business system. The customer focuses the holonic network. Each customer can move from being a consumer to a prosumer. Prosumers contribute by various degrees to the design of the product they request. They are proactive customers that work with the sellers to define the products and services they are buying. Through the design process, the customer forces the network to configure itself to provide the optimum processes to meet his needs. In this way holonic networks go beyond Business Process Reengineering in that they define for the first time how to sell customer-specific products while realizing economies of scale.

The holonic business system is thus the first in which the materials management system is driven real-time entirely by computer.

In a holonic network, continuous improvement occurs at the network level because the network is constantly improving the coordination and communication between nodes. And at the individual node level, each node is constantly improving its core competencies. But within any one virtual company, only nodes that operate at the "best practice" level participate. The only way to improve a virtual company is to remove one or more of the nodes and replace them with "better" nodes. This is tantamount to creating a new virtual company. This is what we mean by the network constantly configuring itself to present the best core business processes in virtual companies.

Within a holonic network, each holon is unique and is unable by itself to create a BreakPoint in the market. Only the power of the virtual company formed of nodes within the holonic network can create a BreakPoint.

In our earlier book on BPR (Johansson *et al.*, 1993), we cautioned readers not to confuse core business process with core technology. We also suggested companies should concentrate on bringing their core business processes to the "best practice" level, or beyond that level to create a BreakPoint opportunity. In a holonic network it is necessary, both to work on improving the core competence of network holons and on their core business processes.

In a single company BPR model, the marketplace does not "know what it wants." It is only through a design of experiments that a company can decide what is most important to the marketplace. In this, a company asks the market "If we could provide you, for example, with three of the following eight characteristics, which three would you like?" In the holonic business system, by contrast, each prosumer knows what he wants, and therefore the virtual company knows the BreakPoint needed by its customers. Going beyond Business Process Reengineering, it is possible to see how with the holonic business system, small companies can compete with large companies. Also, large companies can become cost competitive with small businesses.

Take, for example, the nine-day house built by the Japanese company Sikisui. The customers, a wife and husband, enter the sales office to buy a home. There they find several computer terminals, each linked to company's design office. First, the couple designs the house's basic layout, restricted only by building codes and the size of the lot the house will be built on. Then they begin to personalize it.

They discuss options, with or without the help of the sales agent. They try out "what if's" on the screen. Eventually, they devise a plan that meets their exact specifications. The sales agent offers them tea while they wait for their quotation to be ready, including the cost of building the house. The couple agree to the quotation, and come to terms on a payment schedule. The contract is signed.

Within minutes, the company has sent orders to all of its suppliers to prepare the materials for this custom designed house. If a supplier of one item cannot fulfil its order within three days, it is responsible for finding another vendor in the network of suppliers who can.

Two days before the house is to be built on the customer's site, the components of the house are at the building company's factory. Here they are assembled into modules. Sikisui, with its sales staff and design centers, acts as the integrator in this holonic network that includes dozens of suppliers. Each home—designed by the prosumer—is supplied by a different group of suppliers—in effect a different virtual company for each product. Fifty percent of the parts in the typical home are ordered on a kanban system (i.e. they are repetitive orders), while the other 50 percent are special orders for each home.

That the Sikisui holonic network is effective can be attested by the fact that annual revenues per Sikisui employee are almost $1 million each.

This kind of process can only take place within a network of companies that work with real time communications tools. The user interface software enables the customer to design his or her own product.

This ability to "mass customize" a product from standardized components combines leading technology and communication with preindustrial treatment of the customer. The history of customer relations is the history of industrialization.

The preindustrial craftsman or artisan involved his customer in designing the product itself. Industrialization focused on standardization of goods and of quality. The textiles that came out of early nineteenth-century England and New England factories were the same yard after yard after yard, with no variation due to the particular weaver.

Henry Ford defined twentieth-century standardization when he said that anyone could get any car, so long as it was black. While there was a seller's market—not enough capacity to meet product demand—manufacturers could produce their wares "in black" and they would be purchased.

But after the Second World War, when worldwide capacity began to come into line with worldwide demand, manufacturers began to capture market share by differentiating their product in new ways. For years, cost had been the defining element, then quality. Today after-market service and active consumer participation are the keys. If the basis of competition were not service and participation it would be solely cost. This would further erode margins and stifle growth.

Why has there been such a significant movement since the 1950s to meeting the demands of customers? After all, customers have had needs and desires for centuries. In preindustrial times, artisans worked one-on-one with customers. The customer played an active role in defining what the artisan would make.

Industrialization and mass production "forced" the customer to take what was available. And customers were mostly pleased to oblige; industrialization raised income and living standards to a point where there were plenty of customers for whatever industry could provide. Everyone wanted a washing machine— and did not care if it was large, ugly or inefficient.

The technological leaps of the post Second World War years have given the industrialized world excess capacity. For example, an engineer in 1994 can design and detail ten times as quickly as in 1970. And advanced manufacturing equipment can produce ten times as much product as then—with fewer people operating the machines. Manufacturing management techniques such as Just-in-Time and Total Quality added to overcapacity by making manufacturing operations even more effective and efficient.

The recession of the late 1980s and early 1990s throughout the industrial world only added to the overcapacity. And many Third World markets, which economists had hoped would emerge, simply have not done so. Estimates from the United Nations Development Office are that in real terms GNP per head and real incomes were lower in sub-Sahara Africa in 1993 then in 1970.

Throughout the 1990s corporate restructuring and downsizing—some of it due to companies thinning out through successful BPR efforts—has reduced employment and mothballed production facilities. But there is still excess capacity throughout the system.

In such a "buyer's" market as opposed to the "seller's" market of the industrial period until the 1980s, the customer really is king. With quality no longer a real basis of differentiation, companies are forced to compete on price or new product technology. Customers can either search for low price and plain vanilla products, or can become prosumers and demand ever more customization of products and services. The best companies are responding to the point where customized products can be put together for little more cost than generic products.

We doubt that companies banding together will do anything to solve the world's overcapacity problem—holonic networks will probably exacerbate the difficulties. There will even be continued downsizing. Where holonic networks compete, however, it will be on speed, flexibility and response to prosumers. Virtual companies are able to provide customer driven products at less cost than larger, more monolithic companies.

ADVANTAGES OF THE HOLONIC BUSINESS SYSTEM

There are many advantages to operating within a holonic network, among them:

- *Leverage:* There is true synergy achieved by combining the best capabilities of many operations. Small entities can develop the competitive clout of large companies at a fraction of the cost. Also, shared services such as receivables, purchasing and scheduling can be optimized.
- *Speed:* Decision making is streamlined. There are no layers of management, so no need to sell ideas up the management ladder. Information moves through all forms of telecommunication (most notably electronic data interchange (EDI)). Businesses that are able to act as nodes in a virtual company have had their core competence "prequalified" by the holonic network. Each holon brings to each virtual company as it is established a core competence that it alone manages. Thus, decisions are as rapid as saying "yes" or "no" to the questions: "Do you want to join this virtual company?" and "Do you have the capacity now to join this virtual company?"

  This speed shows up as "time to market," because one company does not have to "invent" an entire new product. It can call on a host of partners with their own core competencies to create a virtual company and to design the new product. It can also show up as "speed to customer," since the virtual company establishes the most effective production core business process.
- *Flexibility:* Coupled with speed is the ability to change the service or product capabilities to match rapidly changing market requirements.
- *Shared risk:* Because several nodes form a holonic network, there is shared risk and reward. There is also a reduction in the fear of change, since each holon is confident in its capabilities. It is not always second-guessing the competition

to see who is developing new capabilities or distinctive product characteristics. In the sense that a holonic network may have several holons that have similar core competencies, sharing risk means that each node can lay off excess work. A node would do this if it were temporarily out of capacity. However, such a decision remains transparent to the customer. Companies are thus not faced with the option of either turning down work—and maybe never being asked again—or working everyone to the bone or hiring new workers who may need to be laid off again when the virtual company ends.

- *Independence:* While the holonic business system requires a great deal of cooperation, there is also the sought-after sense of independence. Each holon is independent, free to come and go as it pleases and to compete and cooperate as it wants.
- *Faster growth and increased profits:* Stalk and Hout found that companies that are one-third more responsive to their customers had a growth rate of three or more times their competition and were two–five times more profitable.
- *Sustainable customers:* Once customers have become used to the flexibility and responsiveness of a holonic system as their supplier, it will be tough for competitors to wean them away. What is more, these customers are often willing to pay a premium for the service.
- *Less capital requirement:* Throughout the holonic network, there is significantly less capital requirement. This is because each node only uses equipment that is specific to its core business processes. All of the non-core process equipment that was previously partially used is now the responsibility of another node. This, in turn, translates into a requirement for less working capital, lower maintenance costs, higher return on assets (ROA), and considerably fewer fixed assets.
- *Quick failure recognition:* Since the network operates in real time it should recognize failures quickly. A well-designed network will have an exit strategy that can be put into effect quickly. The network should be able to be disbanded without damaging the reputation or image of any node. For instance, CFM International is a 50–50 joint venture between General Electric and the French jet engine manufacturer Snecma.

The venture has been in operation since the mid-1970s. The agreement under which it operates allows either company to pull out any time it wants to with no recourse and no recriminations. This may happen if the venture outlives its usefulness. This is not a true holonic enterprise, but the notion of being able to "pull the plug" with no hard feelings is important. As a corollary, in a holonic network operating with such values, shutdown costs should be low, and not detrimental to any node.

● *Increased ability to deal with inevitable change:* Again an example of a joint venture provides valuable lessons. Digital Equipment Company's founder and then president, Kenneth Olson, thought PCs were a "toy" when they were introduced in the early 1980s. By the mid-1980s these "toys" were a significant market. DEC was unprepared to participate in the market on its own and formed a venture with Tandy, the low cost manufacturer of Radio Shack products. Along came Compaq, which offered higher performance to the market. DEC, forced to compete on the performance plane, reconfigured its alliance, adding Intel as a partner in the development of its next generation of PCs. Then came Dell into the market, which offered both low cost and good performance. DEC dropped the alliance with Tandy and began manufacturing on its own. This was a mistake as it turned out, and in practice was also directly contrary to the PC industry's trend towards holonic networks.

A VARIETY OF NETWORKS

There are several different types of holonic networks, often defined by how they come about:

● Vertical networks
● Horizontal networks
● Regional networks
● Out-of-necessity networks
● Self-promoted networks.

Vertical Networks

These most closely resemble what we think of as the traditional supply chain. Usually one node adds some value to an object and passes it off to another node, which in turn adds value, and so on down the value chain.

But within the virtual company there are differences from the traditional model. Automotive OEMs used to be vertically integrated. For example, General Motors still makes almost every subassembly in GM shops, and those it cannot make are made by suppliers quasi-dedicated to them. In this way GM maintains control, GM's leverage over the supplier is the fear of losing GM as a customer. Chrysler, at its peak, was 60 percent vertically integrated. However, today Chrysler has a goal to be only 30 percent vertical, with the rest of subassembly production passed to suppliers working in holonic networks. The unique approach that Chrysler has adopted is to take advantage of its platform engineering to integrate suppliers, assemblers, marketers and design engineers into one cohesive team.

Chrysler has long had a presence in Mexico. With the advent of NAFTA this market is projected to rise from 700 000 vehicles sold within Mexico in 1992 to 1.8 million units well before the turn of the century. For many reasons, political and economic, Mexican suppliers have not kept pace with world standards. In the past Chrysler has tried to overcome these practices by offering equity positions to suppliers. In this manner the supplier became dependent on Chrysler, in much the same way as the *Kieretsu* model works in Japan.

But Chrysler has changed to an idea of "shared destiny," where suppliers actively support the platform engineering concept. Furthermore, Chrysler recognizes that the supplier, in developing the design and technology, owns that part or subassembly design. Therefore, Chrysler encourages the supplier to sell to Chrysler's competitors so that the supplier can maintain economies of scale.

Horizontal Networks

These are networks in which all nodes have the same core competence and share capacity back and forth.

This type of network exists to a large extent in the textile and clothing industry. Here large retail companies order large blocks of items—more than any supplier who receives the contract can deliver in the short period given. To meet demand, the supplier lays off parts of the order onto preselected competitors, creating a system of co-opetion. The relationships are usually reciprocal within a small group of companies.

Regional Networks

Especially common in northern Italy, these networks are created by large groups of small companies. In Italy, the average company has about 45 employees. To handle orders of any size, these companies form tight partnerships with other entrepreneurs. Over time they have come to specialize in small, discrete parts of the value chain.

They are common in the clothing and jewellery manufacturing industries, and in agriculture. Regional governments since the 1980s have sought to create such networks in other industries, including tourism.

Because they were formed in a time when transportation and communications were more difficult than today, being regional in nature was essential. Today, they use their regionalism—their close cultural alliance in both a business sense and a social sense—as a great strength. The best of these alliances are also capitalizing on communications and transportation technologies to make these alliances more powerful than ever.

Out-of-necessity Networks

These networks are often populated by small companies that do not have the capital to develop a market or product. For example, a group of seven small cabinet-making companies pooled their collective expertise to develop a computer numerical control (CNC) router that has become their core technology. Their collective goal was to produce a machine that would cost in the $30 000–$70 000 range. Previously, $200 000 machines were necessary to do the work but had more bells and whistles than any of the small companies needed.

Not only can the seven companies manufacture their finished products more effectively, but by pooling their capital they can expand into new product lines. Moreover, by acting as holonic partners, they can specialize more closely in the components they are best at making, and work for each other. Eventually, they hope to sell the router technology to other competitors.

Self-promoted Networks

These are really single nodes that have a core competence and seek partnerships with other nodes. In each case the company has defined a strategic direction that sets the company's mission to be a node in as many holonic networks as possible irrespective of the ultimate consumer product being made.

These companies live and die on their ability to be a node. An example of such a node is the American Express Purchasing Card Division. It seeks to set up relationships with as many companies as possible and to be a provider of specific services. The Erie Bolt Company has partially given up manufacturing bolts and screws for the hardware market. It now sells its technology and competence in turning, milling, and other activities that go into manufacturing any part that requires screw thread type operations.

TOWARDS THE HOLONIC ENTERPRISE

In this book, we discuss the way such holonic networks and the virtual companies within them come about. Sometimes this is out of design, but more often it happens as corporate executives are pulled increasingly along through competition, technological change and their own reengineering efforts.

Chapter 2 describes in greater detail some holonic networks formed around the world, and defines the boundaries of holonic networks.

Chapter 3 discusses core competencies and how to find them, then how to capitalize on them when looking for opportunities to work with other companies in holonic business systems.

In Chapter 4 we look at the "ways of working" within holonic networks. This includes a look at how companies that do not operate that way today might create the right corporate culture to do so.

Chapters 5 and 6 look at the heart and soul of the holonic business system. In Chapter 5 we look at the ideas of "co-makership," also known as co-op contracting or supplier partnership, and also demand-driven logistics. It is only by creating a fully recognized partnership with suppliers throughout a product's entire value chain that a virtual company can function. Demand-driven logistics is the mechanism by which suppliers acting as partners in a co-makership relationship move goods down the value chain to the consumer.

In Chapter 7, we tackle the issues of what life will be like for individuals working in a business that is a node within a holonic network. Businesses need to think through issues including career paths and compensation. They must consider what happens as employees cross corporate borders to follow a core business process that is being undertaken by a multitude of different corporate entities.

In Chapter 8 we look at how companies that are setting as their strategic direction to be engaged in holonic networks are "selling" themselves and their core competence to other holons in the network.

2
Holonic Principles

As we enter the latter 1990s, it is still difficult to find a group of companies that are working as a true and complete holonic network. What we most often find today are pieces of holonic networks. Groups of companies have put together working arrangements that embody many principles of the holonic business system. In addition, even where networks have not even been formed according to holonic principles, we see many businesses beginning to create holonic style relationships. The most obvious examples are businesses that outsource support or management processes.

Because of this activity, we can say that holonic networks need to have X or Y core competence or capability. We know that only those networks that create and maintain those capabilities and core competencies will be able to maintain a full-scale holonic network over time.

FINDING THE HOLONIC BOUNDARIES

Let us look at an example of two holonic networks doing business at the beginning of 1994, see how they came about and what they are striving to do.

CALIFORNIA TEST BUREAU: CREATING A SINGLE VIRTUAL COMPANY

The California Test Bureau (CTB) came to its holonic network from the perspective of a single company engaging in a rigorous

BPR exercise. CTB discovered that others could conduct many of its support and management processes more effectively. At first glance, this appeared a simple case for outsourcing. But when examined more closely it can be seen that CTB has actively applied the principles of virtual companies and holonic networks. In this way it has created a new organization that has the capacity for growth and change.

CTB provides local school districts throughout the United States with norm-referenced and customized criterion referenced tests for school children. The tests range from kindergarten through grade 12. The company is a division of McGraw-Hill School Publishing Co., which is in turn a division of McGraw-Hill Inc. CTB has 28 percent of the US market for such testing. A competitor has about the same share, and a second competitor a few percent less share. A few small companies cover the last 20 percent of the market and include some states, which produce the tests themselves for intrastate referencing. Current federal legislation mandates such testing, with national norm-referencing, for any school system that wishes to receive federal funds.

CTB, recognized nationally for its leadership in psychometrics, draws up the formulations that decide the validity of the normative results. Unfortunately, the company had a poor turnaround time, and reports did not always reflect the first time exactly what the customer ordered.

The company did most of its business in a very small time-window in the spring. It administered 65 percent of tests between Easter and the third week of May. That put considerable pressure on the scoring and reporting staff, who must complete their work before the end of the school year. This is around the third week of June in the US. Because of the seasonality, there has traditionally been an influx of semiskilled labor to move the test booklets through the scoring process. Compounding that problem, in 1993 it had been decided to close an East Coast scoring facility. This meant consolidating all scoring at the California headquarters, which increased the volume there by 80 percent.

The scoring process is more complex than one would imagine. There are about 100 different tests, each with as many as five different subject areas covered. Most tests are also given in Spanish. There are over 500 report options. The standard report order form alone measures 7½ inches by 14 inches, and is five pages long.

Since the school districts control the testing process CTB never knew when a package of tests would appear, or what the customer would order for reports. Boxes of tests simply appeared and started into the process. Little wonder that an initial evaluation of the process showed a first-pass-yield of 0 percent.

Under the traditional scoring process, boxes of tests appeared at Receiving, where they were opened and checked for an order form and class list. Also a "reasonableness check" was done to see that the proper number of booklets was there, etc. If something was missing—often the case—Customer Service was alerted so it could contact the customer and sort the problem out. Meanwhile, the box was put aside.

The next step was to log the material in. The order form was checked for completeness, and the reporting formats recorded. This was necessary for the report department that developed the job control package to use when generating reports. Again, if there was a problem, Customer Service was contacted for a resolution.

Test booklets were then put through high speed scanners (8000 pages per hour). These read "bubbled in" multiple choice answers and the machine readable class list prepared by the Log-in group. The scanner output was on tape, which was then read and edited by a complex computer program. The edits and the test sheets were sent to the Update group, who manually matched the test sheet with any error messages. By reading the test sheet they could correct any input errors.

Once the grades and school districts were complete, the report writer programs generated the normed report. The reports were checked for completeness, bound and shipped back to the schools. Test booklets were stored for six months and then disposed of.

The process took an average of 30 days from receipt to report shipment. Reruns averaged 15 percent before customers were satisfied with the reports.

Because of the large number of temporary employees, CTB thought that strict compartmentalization and functionalization would enhance efficiency. But this caused isolation, and a lack of any sense of ownership by any CTB employee.

In July 1993 CTB ran a series of customer focus groups, through which they discovered their disgruntled customer base. Customers were finding it harder to justify staying with the company just because of its psychometric purity. Something had to be done, both to maintain the customer base and to better position the company to gain market share.

Dave Taggart, the division President, with the urging and backing of the corporate CFO, undertook to reengineer the scoring process. The first step, as with any reengineering effort, was to map and understand the existing process.

Analysis of the process as it was then practiced showed that only 18 percent of the steps were either value adding or could not be avoided. Value adding process time was only 2 percent of total time. And there was a total of 35 handoffs from one function or activity to another.

CTB formed a team to reengineer the process. It consisted of a representative from each function affected, and the vice president of marketing. The group reasoned that it had to solve the received input problems first. It developed the idea of process teams that would "own" preassigned customers. Also, it developed and fine-tuned the idea of "pre-work."

During the slack time of year, process team members called all of their particular customers to introduce themselves. They also found out which tests were to be given, when they would be arriving at CTB for scoring, and the reporting requirements. They also requested class and school lists. CTB converted the lists when they arrived into machine readable form. They then returned them to the school ready for inclusion in the box of test booklets. Report control cards and invoice controls were prepared beforehand.

This resulted in the ability to treat every class's test returns as a separate case. It is no longer necessary to maintain the cumbersome batch integrity at the district level. Each class test was scored as a separate entity, and the computer sorted the input to aggregate the test results for schools and districts.

With this accomplished, tests speeded through the process. This effort also eliminated the multiple handling of stacks and queues of materials awaiting problem resolution.

For the most part, the physical operations stayed the same. However, the process floor was relayed out so each of the nine teams had its own work benches, scanning machines and update cells. Temporary labor still manned the cells.

Beginning in the spring of 1994, when a box hits Receiving, the appropriate process team is immediately notified. It is the team's responsibility to assure rapid and flawless test processing. Since team members have all the school districts' requirements predetermined, there is no need to contact the schools for additional information. The team can instruct the cell workers immediately on any special processing needs, of which there are still many.

If unusual demand hits one team, cell workers can be temporarily reassigned, just as in a factory operating under the Just-in-Time Uniform Plant Load (UPL) concept. Kanban carts control the overall flow between major operations. Preliminary results showed that a 5–10 day throughput was readily achievable. Furthermore, first pass yield was 78 percent, obtained after overcoming some learning curve glitches by team members. The goal was 95 percent first pass yield.

After the launch of the scoring process teams, Dave Taggart turned the company's attention to the test development process. Traditionally, the testing industry rolls out a new series of standardized tests every seven to eight years. Taggart thought that if CTB could introduce a new test every five years at a total cost per test development 20 percent below the current cost, the company would have a real BreakPoint in the marketplace.

Mass Customization

Taggart's thoughts were completely counter to the reality then, which was causing more costly and longer test development times. This was partially because the market was requiring more customization in tests both at the pedagogy and the population sensitivity levels.

In pedagogical terms, many state departments of education developed curriculums that reflected what they believed are critical skills they want students to master.

For instance, one state may place emphasis on cognitive skills while another may want mastery in analytical skills. No one standardized test is going to satisfy both states. Many states or school districts would put out to bid development and scoring of customized tests. These tests were both costly to the states and low margin business for the companies.

As for population sensitivity, states were increasingly calling on testing companies to show sensitivity to regional and cultural differences in the test question narratives. For example, CTB lost a bid to do the tests for St Paul, Minnesota, because it did not have any references to Vietnamese individuals in the test. St Paul has a large Vietnamese population. As for cultural differences, the state of Iowa may want more agrarian references in arithmetic questions in place of counting city blocks. Many inner city school districts will want to see more multicultural references.

A way had to be found to adapt easily and economically any test to the customer's specific pedagogic or population needs.

Multiple Choice Questions

Look at the typical lower grade level mathematics question, shown in Figure 2.1.

It is not difficult to see that any reasonable guess would lead the student to the answer "G" in the multiple choice format. Critics of multiple choice tests argue that any student would have a 25 percent chance of getting each question right merely by guessing. (There are routines in the scoring/edit program that detect random guessing, although they are not fail-safed.)

F	20
G	70
H	200
J	400

Figure 2.1 Multiple choice question. The picture shows 10 marbles covering the bottom of a 1-liter jar. About how many marbles would fill the jar? F, 20; G, 70; H, 200; J, 400

However, scanning technology can only operate in a multiple choice format. The company's response over time to critics of multiple choice was to create a mixed format test—part multiple choice questions and part "constructed response," which was hand corrected by qualified teachers.

Not only is this approach expensive and time consuming, but it leaves open the question of test corrector bias, or inconsistent grading across grades. Some measures can be taken to reduce these criticisms, but they cannot be fully eliminated. It is also more difficult and expensive to statistically norm the constructive responses.

Resource Availability

In the past, CTB would try to recruit as many as 75 item question writers each time they developed a new set of tests. These were mostly retired school teachers who lived near the Monterey, California headquarters.

These question writers were on the payroll for between one and two years, and not needed again for four or five years. It became increasingly hard for the company to find 75 qualified item writers with the right mix of teaching experience for every test development cycle. This is because high school teachers cannot write questions for third graders. The company had the same difficulty each spring finding short-term help to grade constructive responses.

Toward the Holonic Network

Again, the test development process mapping suggested all together too many handoffs, considerable rework, and ownership of the process only at the top level of the organization.

The process was characterized by many functional departments, each with a small area of responsibility. Further, there were blurred lines between one department's responsibility and the next. And the development tasks were sequential.

The whole process took 6.6 years. A breakdown of the time showed that 32 percent was spent writing and rewriting questions, developing art work and pasting up pages. A full 55 percent of the time was spent in sample acquisition. This consisted of testing questions on small groups of students for difficulty, bias and contribution to score accuracy: 200 000 students took the tests in the fall and again in the spring to create norms across the school year.

Hand scoring, tabulating the results and writing the computer programs for scoring took another 13 percent of the time.

It was determined early in the reengineering effort that the sample acquisition phase could not be improved because of the required tryout and test time constraints. By reengineering the process and establishing multifunction test development teams that worked together in a cell, the other phases could be reduced in time by 37 percent. This was the same as a 19 percent reduction in total time and a 22 percent reduction in cost. The cost reduction came mostly from employing advanced publishing software and the recognition that layers of supervision were not required using the team approach.

While the savings and time reduction were impressive and on their own would have achieved a BreakPoint, that is not the whole story. The reengineering team defined a new level of tests. Through a series of Quality Function Deployment (QFD) sessions with sales people and customers, the reengineering team confirmed the market's direction. It seemed to be moving toward mass customization and away from multiple choice questions.

The team conceived a multidimensional relational data base that would contain all types of different items and stimuli. Stimuli are the basis for a series of items (i.e. an essay followed by a group of questions about the essay's content).

When CTB received a customer request for any form of customization, they could use the data base for developing a specific test.

As often happens in an intensive Business Process Reengineering effort, there is a magic moment when a team's effort seems to coalesce, when the frustration and fatigue break. Some people call it the "aha" moment, when you snap your fingers and say, "Aha that is the key."

For the CTB team, that moment occurred over a working supper of pizzas when someone asked what the data base should be called. "MOMI" was the response of one team member, who like two-thirds of the group was a working mother.

"We'll call it the Museum of Modern Items (a play on the Museum of Modern Art, or MOMA, in New York). It is just like us; MOMI knows all, cares all, can do all and can solve any problem."

Any doubts about creating such a data base were dispelled at that moment. With the creation of MOMI and the need for small batch printing, new sources had to be found. The current printing contractors were all high speed, large batch oriented businesses. And there had to be more than one source, since the capacity required would exceed most small batch print shops.

Two printers were found eventually and each agreed to "sell" CTB capacity for a fast turnaround. By buying capacity, CTB could specify their printing needs a few days ahead of time, and not have to wait in a printer's queue. The company "owned" a slot with each printer every other day.

Next CTB tackled the issue of multiple choice questions. In recent years, imaging technology has been able to achieve higher and higher input speeds. The team reasoned that by converting to imaging, it could produce tests that eliminated the multiple choice format but still retain statistical validity in the testing process. Imaging technology would give students greater flexibility of response.

Figure 2.2 shows the marbles-in-the-glass question as posed in a test that can be graded by a computer that images the pages rather than one that merely scans the bubbles of multiple choice responses. The student writes the answer in the space allowed. Any answer between, say, 50 and 90 would be considered accurate. Not only is this answer more realistic—the spread

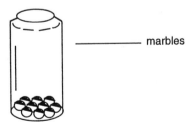

Figure 2.2 *Question marked by computer imaging. "The picture shows 10 marbles covering the bottom of a 1-liter jar. About how many marbles would fill the jar?"*

between 20 and 200 practically forced a multiple choice "guess" of 70—but the student can display spatial relationship reasoning and addition skills in this format.

Imaging also provides for variable page formats and for more supplemental illustrations. This more closely resembles student textbooks. Imaging is also more appropriate for constructed response scoring, and helps scoring done outside CTB offices. CTB sends images by modem to scorers working anywhere in the country. They send back their test results by modem to CTB's mainframe.

But imaging equipment is three to four times more expensive than scanning equipment. The technology is also much more complex, and is rapidly changing. CTB decided to abandon its own technology. It stopped considering imaging as a part of its core business process and as a core competence that needed maintenance. A decision was made to outsource all of the imaging to a company that does only imaging.

Finally, the reengineering team realized that in order to populate the MOMI data base the company would need far more item writers than it could ever hope to get locally. So the company has prepared an instruction manual on how to write items from stimuli—the skill being tested. The company then contracted with scores of teachers around the country who want to freelance in their spare time and during the summer. The company is able to match more closely the freelancers' background and teaching level with the questions they are asked to write. CTB hopes this will reduce the amount of rewriting and shorten the preliminary correction phase.

Many teachers who write questions will use those very same questions to test their students in future years. This is an example of prosumerism at work, with the "client" designing the product.

A Recap of Principles

At the risk of overkill, it might be helpful to reiterate the holonic principles shown in the story of CTB. First it is significant that CTB has managed to provide customer-specific products while realizing economies of scale. The CTB case also illustrates other common features of holonic networks:

1 Successful BPR usually precedes holonic networking, and an excellent BPR effort almost invariably demands holonic networking.

2 Mass customization often forces new technology requirements, which are best obtained from holonic partners rather than trying to add, maintain or upgrade from old technologies in-house. Existing technologies, even after reengineering, are never sacred and must be constantly challenged.

3 Customer involvement, even if not to the level of "prosumerism," can reduce costs and provide expanded market share. Prosumers drive holonic networks.

4 Capacity management at the node level provides the flexibility required of mass customization and the rapid throughput time for responsiveness.

5 There is almost no room for supervisory overheads in a holonic network.

6 Information technology integrates and enables the holonic network. The holonic business system, which goes beyond Business Process Reengineering, is the first to be truly dependent on information technology.

7 Every successful reengineering effort must have a figurative "MOMI"—a breakthrough in thinking that allows the group to grasp the future and "run with it."

THE FOUR ROLES OF HOLONIC PARTNERS

Holonic nodes can fill four different roles within a virtual company.

First is the operational node role. An operational node is one that brings a core competence to a part of the virtual company. These nodes combine along the value chain to produce the physical product that the end customer or prosumer buys.

A second type of node provides support or management processes such as accounts payable, purchasing, quality assurance, information technology, maintenance, accounting and training. These nodes tend to be functionally oriented and there is usually only one per virtual company: one node supports all operational nodes.

The third node plays the role of resource provider, principally to the operational nodes. These resources may be people (skilled temporary labor), buildings, information or finance.

Finally, the fourth type of node role acts as the integrator— the "holon" that unifies the operational and resource nodes' activities. The integrator node may also perform operations, or provide resources. Equally, it may do neither. Its function is to manage and coordinate all of the virtual company's activities.

The integrator can be positioned anywhere in the value chain. CTB does operations such as designing test and results reports. It also functions as the integrator of many test writers and test correctors.

Any of the four types of nodes may be responsible for starting or initiating a holonic network. For Commemorative Wood, the initiator was the distributor who set up a virtual company shortly after Bill Clinton was elected President of the United States in 1992. The sole purpose of the network is to sell small wooden plaques with a photo of Clinton, his political highlights and his signature. All of the nodes in the virtual company were small shops in Arkansas, the President's home state. One wood shop glued together previously discarded scrap oak pieces to form a block; a second shop formed the blanks into plaques. Yet another printed the artwork and shipped it to a fourth. This shop applied the artwork to the block it had received, finished the plaque, and sent it to the distributor.

Another type of initiator is the "major player," such as Ford or Chrysler in its development of "system selling," discussed in greater detail in Chapter 8 of this book. Here they sought to go beyond Business Process Reengineering toward a holonic network to allow them as a large company to compete successfully with small companies. Ford supported its suppliers to expand their contribution to product development and production of subsystems.

Still other holonic networks developed "from the front end of the line." Allied Fibers created such a network when it created Carpetnet, described in detail in our previous book (Johansson *et al.*, 1993).

Whatever the reason, the key for the initiator of a holonic network is to recognize the value it can add for customers. With this knowledge the initiator can sell the idea up and down the value chain. The more that a business has holonic ideas as a part of its strategic thinking, the more it will be receptive to innovation. It does not seem to matter what size the potential nodes are, but that they have positioned themselves to play a part in a holonic network.

We will discuss the initiator and integrator roles in far greater detail in Chapter 7 of this book. They deserve detailed treatment. The success with which the integrator does its work will have a lot to do with the success of each virtual company. Ultimately, the success of the virtual companies affects the success of the holonic network.

What you have in a fully functional holonic network is Process Taylorism. Here the tasks and activities that must take place to accomplish the core business process are broken down into evermore discrete parts. Each node becomes ever more specialized at doing one set of tasks and activities. Taylorism applied at the individual operator or person level without pressure from a virtual company is almost doomed to fall into the trap of suboptimization. This is because the focus within a holonic node is only on improving its core business process. The focus within the virtual company is on upgrading capabilities and on improving the delivery of goods and services through the value chain. Thus by both the node and the virtual company focusing on the process they cover the whole core business process and reduce the danger of suboptimization.

Producing Goods in the Holonic Network

From a manufacturing point of view, the first stage to develop a virtual company is the design process. Virtual companies whose core competence is in product supply can begin manufacturing only when the product design ensures that "personalization" is quick and inexpensive. If the design is modular, manufacturing can exploit it to the fullest, and assembly systems made as straightforward as possible. Recycling also needs to be considered to ensure maximum use is made of each component and that waste is reduced.

There is also the issue of designing for reusability—from plastic bottles to fiber fill for winter ski jackets, plastic park benches and picnic tables.

To be truly effective, manufacturing processes need to take place in computer-linked small-scale units. Information technology and process engineering capabilities must be used to ensure that manufacturing becomes one continuous flow between the nodes and the customers.

Advances in manufacturing technology mean that low cost manufacturing units are now realizable. Factories will in the future be smaller, and more widely dispersed. If factories downsize to handle only the activities in their core business processes, then support and management processes should be cost effectively dispersed to other nodes and customer sites.

The manufacturing node is in many ways the most critical operational node in a product supply virtual company. It is likely to have required the greatest capital investment, and to have the most employees. For that reason, it merits special attention and must aquire a new agility.

The ideas of agile manufacturing are now emerging in the United States backed by the Department of Defense. There are two reasons for this.

First is global uncertainty. With the cold war cancelled, the time, place and nature of threats to American security are difficult to predict. For example, the US Army worked out 1200 scenarios of future conflicts before the Gulf War. Only three of these involved a war in the Persian Gulf, and none of these had Iraq as the antagonist. As the capability to predict future conflicts decreases, the need for a capability to gear up for them increases.

Cost is the second reason. Congress will no longer grant the Pentagon the funds to stockpile vast amounts of material. This means that it may have to manufacture half a million desert boots in a matter of weeks. In times of conflict, agile manufacturing can save lives.

As preparations began for the Gulf War, the Department of Defense saw a need for a way to stop casualties from friendly fire. A team of Department experts went through a pile of proposals. On Wednesday 13 February 1991 they authorized Test Systems Inc. of Hudson, NJ to begin work on an identification beacon. On Saturday, the 16th, a successful test ran with a private aircraft and a "breadboard" version of a beacon on an Army truck. On Sunday, the 17th, manufacture of 10 prototypes began. On Tuesday, less than one week after contract authorization— no doubt the paperwork had yet to be completed—Air Force General M. P. C. Carns, had a working model on his desk. A similar unit was also on its way to Saudi Arabia on an Air Force C-5. By Saturday, just 10 days after authorization, the first 40 production units were on their way to Saudi Arabia.

There are six main ideas behind agile manufacturing, according to Stuart Madnick, Professor of Information Technology at the Massachusetts Institute of Technology, Sloan School of Management.

1 Assimilating information from customers better and faster.
2 Empowering individuals to make decisions.
3 Building high-speed networks for transmitting information.
4 Researching, designing and setting up production simul-taneously, known as concurrent engineering.
5 Tailoring each unit to individual customers' wishes without delaying delivery or increasing costs, known as mass customization.
6 Creating organizations able to re-invent themselves overnight in response to global challenges and opportunities.

A research report titled "21st Century Manufacturing Enterprise Strategy" by the Lehigh University Iacocca Institute, was partly funded by the Department of Defense. In it was the following scenario of manufacturing in 10 to 15 years.

"It is the year 2006. 'US Motors' (USM), a leading agile manufacturer, uses sophisticated information technology to keep a startling promise— delivery of a car within three days of being ordered, configured to the customer's specifications.

Using home computers and modems, potential customers 'dial up' images of cars they are considering, including prices and estimated operating costs. If they wish, customers can experience the car through 'virtual reality' machines at a nearby dealer. Through USMNet, a computer network, consumers get updated information on repair histories of all USM cars, parts, options and estimated labour costs for repairs and servicing.

Another major customer of USM is the Pentagon. Rather than stockpile every imaginable kind of vehicle for every possible global configuration, the Defense Department uses USM's agility to produce vehicles when and where needed, tailored to order.

USM borrows an idea popular with computer makers in the 1980s and encourages third party aftermarket suppliers to offer USM compatible equipment. As computer makers learned, the larger the third party supplier base, the longer the life of the 'platform' (ie USM's car), even when new and more competitive platforms are introduced.

By staying lean and flexible, USM can make small batches of vehicles—say, 60 000—yet still keep costs low and then quickly redesign to stay ahead of competitors' whims. Suppliers are networked with USM, as are dealers, all working together to produce high-value, high-quality products in tune with the changing tastes of car buyers around the world."

In their article in the January/February 1994 *Harvard Business Review,* Robert Hayes and Gary Pisano argue that, too often, companies focus on the "form" of how they are going to compete. For example they will compete by using JIT or TQM. Instead they should focus on the "substance" of how they are going to compete, that is the skills and capabilities that allow a factory to achieve excellence. Hayes and Pisano say that besides choosing their long-range skill set, companies should focus on the "form" of how they will obtain the skill level.

For instance, they say, if a company competes by applying high levels of low cost automation then the road to proficiency will be through computer technology and the data rigors of MRP. If, however, a company is going to compete on speed and flexibility, then the experience and skill of setup reduction and pull systems might be the appropriate approach. Either way, "the key to long-term success is being able to do certain things better than your competition can."

They go on to say, that every company needs "strategic flexibility" to shift ground quickly with minimal resources, for example to move from rapid product development to low cost manufacturing.

Extended beyond a single company, this is exactly the way holonic networks and the virtual companies within them compete, and the way they have to think through strategy.

Setting yourself up as a factory in a holonic network means adopting many ideas of agile manufacturing. It also requires attention to the manufacturing processes and the introduction of such ideas as flexible cells. At the Allied Bendix division that manufactures braking systems these ideas were used to design and manufacture new antilock brake systems in record times. At Texas Instruments one factory manufactures both DRAM memory chips and expensive customized microprocessors. By design, both chips share the same equipment for 90 percent of the production process. Only at the end of the process do the microprocessors get customized. TI maintains that it runs the facility at full capacity by constantly changing the mix to meet demand. They flex the more profitable microprocessor manufacture between 10 and 60 percent of capacity. During high microprocessor demand they outsource the "jelly bean" DRAM to one of 13 other manufacturers.

Behind many ideas adopted in manufacturing nodes lies the idea of a "lot size of one." This is clearly an advantage where manufacture is done to order, since it avoids the creation of potentially unwanted inventory. However, the achievement of this aim is often difficult as it requires significant investment in state-of-the-art process equipment. Some of this, such as flexible manufacturing systems, is computer controlled to reduce setup times. Often a "lot size of one" implies that the product itself must be "design for one" and customer variants obtained in software rather than in hardware. Lot control becomes simpler in that individual units are traceable. However, such a practice increases proportionately the volume of data. Technically, individual units are traceable through manufacturing operations on a smart chip. The MEGA-PC case described this in Chapter 1. There the company used a smart chip to carry manufacturing instructions for its ASICs. Increasingly, the idea of dedicated cells and tooling just will not hack it in the future.

The manufacturing operational node in a virtual company is certain to be on the critical path of delivery reliability. This means that it should make every effort to fail-safe each manufacturing process step. There are several levels of fail-safing sophistication. At the simplest, this may be by next-operation detection or by operator inspection coupled with precontrol. A more sophisticated approach is to use internal adaptive control in the process itself, or predictive control that can be a product or process characteristic. Finally, design for fail-safing can remove more costly production process modifications.

For example, the sides of all stoves in the US are the same size, since they fit into standard kitchen cabinets. It is difficult to tell the right side from the left side, especially during the multiple forming operations. Consequently, the first metal stamping operation includes punching a hole—which eventually becomes a fastener hole for final assembly—in the right panel or side.

The tools for both the right and left sides are fitted with photocells. At a subsequent right-side stamping operation, there has to be a photo connect signal for the press to close. If there is no connect it means that the piece is a left panel and the press will not operate. The opposite logic holds true for left-hand panels.

The ultimate aim is to bring the customer and the manufacturing facility as close together as possible. This reduces transport costs and traffic times. Sometimes, the factories can locate at the sales or distribution center. This is the case with one-hour eyeglasses, where the lens blanks are edged and fitted into frames in a laboratory right in the retail store. Similarly a "hole-in-the-wall" can maker supplying a brewer from right next door eliminates transportation costs.

STARGUEST: PUTTING THE PIECES TOGETHER

In an attempt to increase tourism, the chambers of commerce of the Italian regions of Lombardy and Emilia Romagna launched the Starguest network project in 1994. Starguest is billed as "a holonic international network for the creation, distribution and management of integrated hospitality service for holiday and business travel."

Tourism is a natural enterprise for holonic networks and virtual companies. In the tourism industry, a "virtual product" is one that does not exist until the customer creates it. This demand must be catered for by a virtual company in the travel sector that is begun with the sole purpose of concluding this one item of business. This requires the presence of an almost invisible but highly sophisticated network of infrastructures. This network, founded on the integration of organization and technology, is backed up by a multimedia software system. Such systems are well within the capabilities of current information technology.

Many Italian tourist areas (art cities, coastal and mountain resorts) provide concentrations of independent nodes—hotels, attractions, etc.—to create holonic networks. But to move from potential to reality they need a greater degree of integration and rationalization than now, especially in the area of management.

A truly holonic travel network goes beyond conventional telebooking. Libraries of videos and CD-ROMs help in four fundamental ways:

1 The creative aspect of the holiday is entrusted totally to the customer—with or without any desired assistance. The traveller is the architect of the integrated package rather than the packager or travel agent.
2 A holonic network of companies shares common objectives, and the use of total quality and other management techniques by all participants' work toward attaining the highest possible customer satisfaction. The customer is always the focal point in such a system.
3 An integrated software system allows the customer to self-define the holiday or convention program according to personal taste. Rapid but effective psychographic analysis and a "decision tree" design allow the information system to present choices to the customer. Answers given to preliminary questions enable the choices to be "to the customer's liking." In a well-designed system of this type the customer senses no burden and does not feel "pushed" in any direction. He feels only that the system is always responsive to his or her desires or requirements.
4 The existence in a node, of a low profile but continuous service of assistance and monitoring of customer satisfaction levels throughout the travel period.

Figure 2.3 shows how a typical virtual company within the Starguest network is made up. Looking first at the large circle, in the center is the customer satisfaction system. This is a resource node monitoring customer satisfaction in every virtual company. Every specific holiday or conference transaction requires its own virtual company.

In tourism, the product is the direct experience of the customer. The system that guarantees customer satisfaction therefore coincides precisely with the "core business process" of any company in the travel industry. Any company that works within the tourism industry will define its core business process as

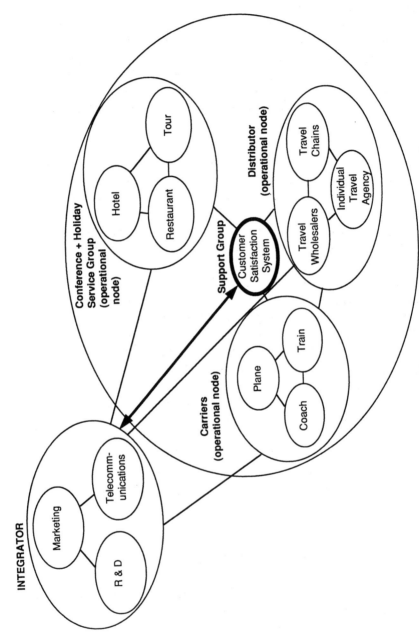

Figure 2.3   *A typical virtual company within the Starguest network*

"providing each customer with the best possible travel (holiday or business) experience."

In the traditional travel industry, every player in the chain of events has its own way of measuring and providing customer satisfaction. These players include the travel agent, the tour operator, the hotel and the air or rail carriers. In the Starguest network, a separate support node carries out this function. It transfers to all nodes throughout the network information about factors that make for customer satisfaction, thus enabling the network to be self-learning.

Around the support node that provides customer satisfaction information are a host of operational holons that provide the tangible services such as transportation, hotel, restaurant and other services. Additional operational nodes provide distributor services which do the actual bookings. These would include travel wholesalers, travel agency chains and individual travel agencies.

Finally, on another plane of activity, is the holonic integrator node which in this example also provides the resources. From the customer satisfaction responses (support node) it can conduct R&D. Essentially R&D means working to enlist other operational nodes into the network and in this way provide added or expanded options for the traveller. Not only can the integrator add nodes; it can also delete the unsatisfactory ones. Additionally it maintains the network's information data base and provides interactive hardware to the operators.

Figure 2.4 shows the way the holonic network was envisioned to operate, as it connects local operational nodes and local customer satisfaction resource nodes to distributed operational nodes in the three main markets of the US, northern Europe and Japan.

TRUST IS THE KEY

Mutual respect and trust build holonic networks. Any node that does not maintain itself as trustworthy will no longer participate in virtual companies that form within the holonic network. This mutuality binds companies together in a shared destiny.

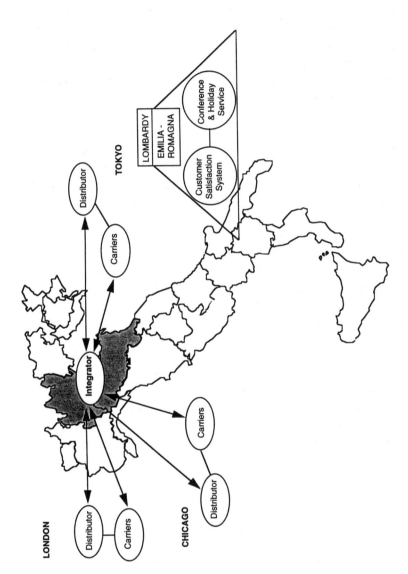

Figure 2.4 *The way in which the holonic network was envisioned to operate.*

Many executives are uncomfortable working with competitors in a relationship of trust. "I know I have to do it, but it goes against everything I was trained to do," said one American corporate CEO in the automotive supplier industry. He was describing his feelings about playing the role of an operational node in a virtual company which was manufacturing a system for an automotive OEM. Here a competitor is the integrator. He is competing fiercely against the same competitor to be the integrator node for a different OEM.

This executive knows that no first tier supplier can do it alone any more. The automotive OEMs need ever more design capability, faster time to market, and best value on each component that goes into a system. To respond to these needs companies must become operational nodes and cease to consider that they must win the integrator role. They must find and trust partners—many of them competitors—to manufacture some of their subassemblies. It is when companies acknowledge a shared destiny that they can enter this kind of trust-based relationship.

Informality and lack of hierarchy characterize holonic networks, there is nothing wrong with each node agreeing to and signing a single page statement of purpose. This could be as simple as the handwritten note written by the heads of Boeing and United Airlines. It was written in a hotel room characterizing both companies' objectives for the development of the Boeing 777. The text of the note read:

> "B777 Objective, United and Boeing. In order to launch on-time a truly great airplane we have a responsibility to work together to design, produce and introduce an airplane that exceeds the expectations of flight crews, cabin crews, and maintenance and support teams and ultimately our passengers and shippers. From day one: Best dispatch reliability in the industry; Greatest customer appeal in the industry; User friendly and everything works. October 1990."

This level of trust is so necessary because of the "apparent chaos" that exists within holonic networks. This apparent chaos is the result of the multitude of information connections that exist in the network. Each node needs to be able to communicate with each other node. It also has contact with the world "outside" the network, to maintain its sensitivity both to the marketplace and to the specific prosumer.

Every individual node has access to the comings, goings and decisions of every other node. It is a completely open system in which any node can present information. Every node is an expert and it has to display a core competence important to the network's activities. It can act on available information as it pertains to its sphere of influence.

This also implies that if an individual company within the network objects to a decision or action it has very little time—a relative nanosecond—to object. Presumably there will be no need to object, since each node is working toward a shared purpose and the actions taken reflect that purpose. This would support the concept that in a truly holonic network there are no leaders or followers, there are only contributors.

This means that for holonic networks to be successful over any length of time, actions taken must be aboveboard. They must be clearly in the best interest of the process rather than in the best interest of any individual node.

3
Capabilities, Competencies and Beyond Business Process Reengineering

When we talk about BreakPoint Business Process Reengineering, we mean the radical improvement of core business processes to improve a company's performance. The term Business Process Reengineering (BPR) has come to include improvements to any business process. These include improvements to support processes and to management processes.

For a company to be able to join as a node in a holonic network, it must have some experience of Business Process Reengineering. Preferably it will have undertaken a BreakPoint BPR effort. There needs to be found in each individual company a combination of aggressive, groundbreaking Business Process Reengineering efforts on the one hand and on the other a cycle of continuous improvement. A business must have instilled within its culture at least the ideas of continuous improvement, even if it does not have a long-active continuous improvement program.

The company will have defined its core business processes and its support and management processes. The company will also have made some progress toward reengineering these processes. Support processes are those that enhance the product in the eyes of the customer, but do not fully meet the criteria for being a core business process. An example of a support process is recruitment. The company makes a statement of its values and beliefs that is read by customers and also by recruits. If it is consistent then it results in securing the best personnel.

Together, the reengineering and continuous improvement efforts will have had a significant impact on the company's customers. The Business Process Reengineering effort will have provided the basis on which the company has configured its activities to maximize both their effectiveness and their efficiency. This will be significant when it comes to complying with the increased demands put on them by prosumers.

CORE BUSINESS PROCESSES

By core business processes, we mean the handfull of processes central to a company's operations that "creates" value for external stakeholders in the business. Core business processes create value for the customer, the shareholder or the regulator and are critical to get right.

Companies usually have about a half dozen or so core business processes. They are the processes that the business's strategic thinking has identified as critical to excel at to meet or beat the competition. They make up part of the company's set of core competencies. A core competence may be a business process, a management skill, a "new" asset or an applied technology.

Gary Hamel, a professor at The London Business School, has determined three tests by which to judge if a capability is a core competence.

1 Does it make a disproportionate contribution to customer value?
2 Does it offer the opportunity to build competitive distinction?
3 Is it applicable in other businesses, locations or products?

Much confusion arises in distinguishing between capabilities and core competencies. The words capability and competence have broadly the same meaning. For example, pediatricians are capable of basic medicine for adults because of their general training, but are competent in medical care for children because of their specialized additional study. We take the view that a core competence is one of the critical subset of capabilities that satisfies

Hamel's test. By our reckoning, because core business processes satisfy Hamel's test, most of the few core competencies of a business will be its core business processes. Besides core business processes, a company's core competencies will include applied technologies or management skills.

A business has to be capable of doing many different things if it is to exist. We consider therefore that capabilities are everything that a business needs to compete: they may be an ability to work in teams; they may be attributes such as knowledge; they may be any an activity that goes on in every business, from receiving visitors at the front-desk to signing off the annual audit. Capabilities can be accidents of history such as the locations of the business's offices and patents. Management capabilities, however, are most in evidence in the style of leadership and communication adopted in the business.

Managers have seemed focused on tearing down corporate boundaries since the idea of Business Process Reengineering emerged. They have sought to change the working practices of their businesses and to align the activities of staff more closely with core business processes. However, the management processes by which they use the human and material resources of businesses have changed very little. As the holonic enterprise emerges from the experiences of Business Process Reengineering things are changing.

The policies and mechanisms that helped the work of management are no longer appropriate in process teams. The structure of organizations in which function and level of responsibility meant that each person was clear on his or her authority and decision-making limits has disappeared.

Instead, self-managed teams introduce confusion and the need for organizational agility. So too, has the work-unit climate changed in the holonic business. Before, it was one in which there was a clear superior-to-subordinate relationship between the boss and his staff. Now it is a flexible relationship in which the most appropriate person always sets direction. Self-managed teams can, however, give the appearance of confusion because their members often have different and sometimes conflicting agendas, sometimes within teams and often across teams. We have visited companies who have set up as many as 15 "teams" in their reengineering effort. Each of these teams was functionally oriented and each had its own conflicting goals. For example, one team was adding distribution centers to "better service the customer." Another team was reducing the planning cycle to decrease inventory. A third was investing in higher speed equipment to make larger lot sizes—all in the name of business process reengineering.

Finally, motivation—the behavioral tendency to move towards a goal and to persist until satisfaction has been achieved—has changed. No longer is the success of the individual business uppermost in the manager's mind but the success of the network and its virtual businesses has increased in importance. In Chapter 7 we discuss loyalty in holonic networks.

In the holonic enterprise leadership is not concerned with command and control, but with the building of core competence. Management's role is not to manage but to remove obstacles not—as often happens—to create them. One example is the way Goran Carstadt, president of IKEA, describes his organization as "upside down." Leadership style is that of coach, mentor and team challenger. If the leaders must focus on something then it should be first on core competencies and not products or services.

Of course a focus on the customers' needs has long been the theme of the Total Quality Management movement. In Business Process Reengineering we began to realize that only those processes that add value to the customer are likely to enable a business to make radical changes. Now, going beyond Business Process Reengineering, it is apparent that merely adding value is insufficient.

The aim of reengineering core business processes is to "impress" the customer and to cause delight. A reengineered process should cause the customer to behave in totally new ways. Consider the impact City Bank's 15 minute mortgage approval process had on its first customers. It must be similar to the delight that filled the eyes of Edwin Land's daughter when he produced the first Polaroid picture minutes after its exposure.

In a holonic network it is necessary to go further than adding value and impressing the customer. It is necessary to influence the way a customer interacts with the virtual company through the processes that it employs. In this way the customer of a virtual company becomes a prosumer, and becomes central to the holonic network.

Lest we confuse the reader, we realize that not all products sold will be directly designed by the customer. It would be silly to think of every customer who eats cereal for breakfast designing their own cereal and package. But, look at the myriad of breakfast cereals available to the consumer today. Some cereals cater to the need for the fanciful to entice a child to eat them. Other cereals emphasize the nutritional values such as high vitamin content. Still others suggest the prophylactic medicinal value of high fiber to reduce the incidence of colon cancer. If the consumer was not "designing" these new offerings we would still be eating Weetabix or Cheerios. The cereal manufacturing and box making operations would be happy because they would have to make a few products with long, "efficient" runs.

Prosumerism is as powerful in the commodity market as it is in the one-off market. Businesses that use this approach go beyond business process rengineering toward the holonic enterprise because they can sell customer-specific products without losing economies of scale.

First, however, you need to concentrate on the core business processes. A team formed to spearhead a reengineering effort should draw a "quickmap," essentially a high-level process map of the core business processes. The quickmap takes a big picture of the processes, bounds it and lays it out. A quickmap gives enough detail to begin the search for targets for reengineering. In a more complex business, it is necessary to decompose the core business processes. This means breaking them down into one or more levels. The decomposition should continue until an activity is found that is discrete enough for a successful reengineering effort.

In a business that has undertaken reengineering, the core business processes will be strongly in evidence for several reasons.

First, they will have increased in importance and become the subject of focused, sustained attention. It is likely that between 20 and 50 percent of the business leader's time will be committed to ensuring the effectiveness and efficiency of the core business processes. Included in this will be time to enhance the capabilities that support them.

Second, the core business processes will have become unconstrained by the availability of resources or assets. These will be freely available. To express this in manufacturing terms, the support processes that supply the core business processes with the "new" assets and other capabilities are considered to have infinite capacity. The "new" assets are available on demand to the core business processes through a pull system.

SUPPORT PROCESSES

Support processes can often be considered as suitable for outsourcing. This is discussed in more detail in Chapter 6. If they remain within the business, they will not be effective or efficient unless they receive the necessary investment to maintain their capabilities. This implies that training and upgrading is essential for those working in support processes. Furthermore, a systematic measurement program is necessary to monitor the effectiveness of the support processes across the whole business.

We have seen many Business Process Reengineering efforts focused on support processes. The success stories of reorganized payment and invoicing systems that result in vastly reduced costs appear in the business press daily. Lest we appear cynical (the definition of a cynic being a disappointed enthusiast) we should stress that such reengineering is vital for the success of companies today. The innovation, process mapping, piloting, process benchmarking and problem-solving techniques of Business Process Reengineering have a strong and valid role to play in these programs. It is hardly, however, the radical change to organizations and industries promised by the reengineering movement.

Support processes are often complex and have multiple handoffs. "Case workers," who can handle complete support processes, are eliminating complex support processes and achieving significant improvements. The ideas of industrial process efficiency, such as P-charts to log percentage failures, are making significant contributions in the administrative and clerical areas. For example, the statistical process control (SPC) charts that enable exception reporting to replace periodic reporting have found a new home in the administrative support groups of many businesses.

In our work with Business Process Reengineering we have seen many businesses, from food manufacturers to computer giants, begin to pilot their efforts with the reengineering of business support processes. We recognize that this provides a ready target and a potential for cash savings. However, it also seems that while the rhetoric of managers is customer value they sign-off on cost reduction.

In a node any activity that is in a support or management process is a candidate for outsourcing to other nodes in the network. Any cost in a core business process is under constant scrutiny. Beyond Business Process Reengineering, then, brings the elements of cost back to the center stage. This is particularly the case for those who have already undertaken a Business Process Reengineering effort and made strides in time, service, quality and product enhancement issues.

MANAGEMENT PROCESSES

Every business also has a third kind of process within its activities—management processes. Having the right kinds of management processes is important in creating a company culture in which reengineering can be successful. Without them a company cannot offer itself to a holonic network. It is not ready for inclusion as a node in virtual companies.

Management processes are concerned frequently with creating the regulatory, legal and financial environment within which the business operates. Management processes include, for example, strategic planning, budgeting, statutory reporting, conducting staff appraisals and doing corporate public relations. A holon may decide to outsource its management processes. However, those that it retains need development if they are not to wither.

This means that all businesses have to consider how to develop their existing capabilities. It may be through such activities as continuing management education, sabbaticals and continual cross-training. It is possible to arrange short-term "trades" of managers with other companies or academia. Executives have been lent to government and the not-for-profit sector.

Managers must accept responsibility for their own training. It has to be as relevant for them and the positions they hold. Without relevance neither managers nor staff will engage in the training. A most important benefit of training is that it involves all managers in the issues facing the company. Management capabilities, however, are most in evidence in the style of leadership and communication adopted within the business.

Management processes are also necessary to develop and deploy measurements within nodes and across nodes. These measures must be appropriate for individuals, teams, processes within nodes and the virtual company.

PROCESS IMPROVEMENT GRID

Business Process Reengineering has become the business idea of the 1990s—the plethora of books, conferences and press articles bear testimony to this. But much of what is touted as reengineering is little more than re-warmed Total Quality, continuous improvement or systems application. Some successful efforts have been undertaken under the name of Total Quality, such as the effort by AlliedSignal.

The name is not as important as what the undertaking really is. We believe that to qualify as true Business Process Reengineering, an effort must focus on improving the way a company operates and this means not just the efficiency with which activities are conducted.

We have come to realize that there are many ways to improve business processes. The difference relates to the level of ambition within a company. We determine ambition by the breadth or scope of a Business Process Reengineering effort across the business, and the scale of improvement—and therefore market impact—sought.

As to scope, Business Process Reengineering can be concerned with improving the efficiency of a single activity in a single function. It can also introduce changes to single core business processes, such as often occurs in supply chain reengineering. This attempts to change logistic processes that cross functional and departmental boundaries. Finally, a Business Process Reengineering effort can seek to redefine the company's entire business system.

The reegineering of single processes in single functions can be important to the business that undertakes it, but it is unlikely to deliver the scale of radical improvement and widespread results that many companies are seeking. Process scope in a Business Process Reengineering effort is critical for two reasons.

First, if a Business Process Reengineering effort includes multiple processes it is more likely to discover the benefits of eliminating handoffs between processes. Second, the speed with which the effort will influence the company's financial results is directly proportional to the number of processes included in the reengineering effort. We have been struck in our work by many attempts to do Business Process Reengineering that fail to provide convincing results. Often this is because they simply were not sufficiently broad and inclusive. There is a critical mass of processes necessary for success.

As for scale, there are three possible reasons for undertaking a Business Process Reengineering effort.

First, a company can undertake Business Process Reengineering for cost reduction. This means it will engage in what we call "process improvement." Process improvement often focuses on support process change in areas such as information services and accounting services. It uses approaches such as subcontracting, outsourcing and facilities management (see Chapter 6).

Second, a company can undertake Business Process Reengineering for the purposes of becoming more competitive, which often requires action in areas other than cost. The company must attempt to reach "best-in-class" status, which means attaining parity with the companies that achieve the best performance in similar core business processes. Efforts such as simultaneous engineering for new product development, supply chain optimization or an intensive Just-In-Time project in a key manufacturing area often achieve best practice.

Third, a company can undertake Business Process Reengineering to rewrite in its favor the rules of competition in its industry or segment. Here change will influence the whole business, resulting in a major shift in market dynamics. We term this BreakPoint BPR. For this, a company will seek to attain a BreakPoint. We define this as the achievement of excellence in one or more of the qualities the marketplace values. The degree of excellence is such that the company gets a disproportionate positive reaction from its marketplace.

To achieve a BreakPoint, it is necessary for a company to find a way to startle the market. Often this means to deliver more

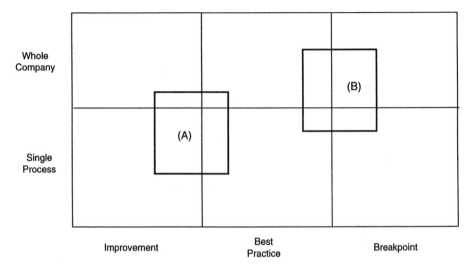

Figure 3.1   *Process improvement grid for a single company*

than customers even think they want. Such an impact is achieved through reengineering one or more of the core business processes in terms of a product value measure: cost, quality, cycle time, delivery, reliability and product innovation. To seek a BreakPoint, extensive marketplace research is necessary. This enables the company to find which of its core business processes could provide a huge leap in market share and marketplace recognition.

These dimensions of scale and scope shown diagrammatically we call the process improvement grid. Figure 3.1 shows the process improvement grid for a single company doing process improvement.

Most companies that undertake Business Process Reengineering efforts do so in the area marked A. Here most of the efforts concern the improvement of a single process for cost reduction and streamlining. A small part of the total effort aims to improve the company's performance. The business undertaking this sort of effort pays little attention to improving core business processes or to becoming a "best practices" company.

The more aggressive, forward-looking companies often undertake their Business Process Reengineering efforts in the area marked B. Here there are attempts made by the company to achieve best practice. These attempts concern individual core business processes.

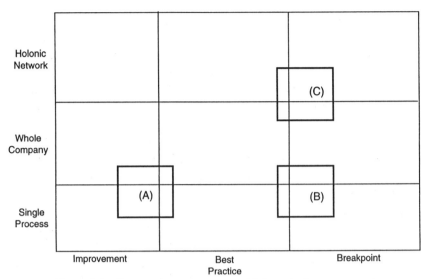

Figure 3.2 *Process improvement grid for a holonic network*

BEYOND BUSINESS PROCESS REENGINEERING

The process improvement grid shown in Figure 3.1 relates to the approaches available to a single business unit in undertaking a process improvement program. We can extend this thinking to a holonic network, as shown in Figure 3.2. Here we can see how efforts to seek at least best practices and often BreakPoints extend beyond the boundary of a single business unit and cross the holonic network.

Companies that are successful nodes within a holonic network continue their Business Process Reengineering efforts, both individually and within their virtual companies. This requires efforts in both the best practices and BreakPoint areas, signified by area C within Figure 3.3.

Because a holonic network by definition configures itself each time it creates a virtual company, it is always working in the best practices and BreakPoint area.

THE DEATH OF THE STRATEGIST

At the heart of so many businesses for the last 40 years is a highly structured approach to strategy formulation. There is no doubt that the rapid configuration of holonic networks to form virtual companies will rewrite these approaches. When the future is desperately uncertain and virtual companies form instantaneously to meet specific prosumers' needs, a business strategy that lays down a rigid framework is inappropriate. We predict, therefore, the death of the business strategists as we know them today because of the emergence of holonic networks.

In the traditional strategy formulation process, products, markets and regions were decomposed and segmented into ever narrower groupings. The basic idea behind this decomposition was "focus," and the logic went as follows.

Analyze the areas of competition that are addressable by the business unit and within these the characteristics on which the business unit can successfully differentiate itself and compete. Based on the analysis, synthesize the important niches and focus on them. Test this focused strategy with a financial model to see if it gives acceptable returns to shareholders. If so, end activities that do not fit into the new focus and invest in those that do.

Unfortunately, this kind of tunnel visioning or focus has a significant weakness in that it fails to find performance break-throughs that can extend a product or a market. By its very nature the approach defines and conserves existing niches. Furthermore, it will rarely suggest creating or discovering new products or markets outside the company's existing technologies. Today, nothing characterizes a successful business more than its willingness to abandon the reasons for its success. Managers must approach the future more creatively to create new niches and rearrange established ones. Nonetheless, most managers remain entranced by the promise of long-range planning in the same way that they will consistently cross the street rather than walk under a ladder.

When strategies do consider new products and markets, they are constrained by their company's current perspective. In a holonic network the nodes can come together, each with a different perspective, to aid in the strategic thinking process. This process develops synergy between the nodes and can be considered as a "synergy of values."

In his book, *The Rise and Fall of Strategic Planning*, Henry Mintzberg (1994) shows how inappropriate the traditional approaches to strategy formulation have become. Mintzberg, a

McGill University professor and former president of the Strategic Planning Society, makes the argument that strategic planning is a fundamental contradiction in terms, that is as it has been defined to predict rationally and control the future.

Mintzberg is not alone, As Brian Quin of Dartmouth University has said, "A good deal of corporate planning is like a ritual rain dance. It does not affect the weather that follows, but those who engage in it think it does. Moreover, much of the advice directed at corporate planning relates to improving the dancing, not the weather." Mintzberg gives many rational and compelling reasons to believe that corporate strategic planning is no longer appropriate. He shows how in a rapidly changing world over-reliance on historic hard data—the bread and butter of corporate strategists—can only lead to wrong conclusions. The only thing that is certain about the world of tomorrow is that it will be different from today and yesterday. Further, he argues that businesses, their processes and their markets cannot be logically decomposed for strategic analysis since today's processes and markets are interdependent.

Our experience in Business Process Reengineering confirms Mintzberg's argument. A change in any process will affect all the other processes in the business.

While Business Process Reegineering is tactical rather than strategic in nature, it does lead to new strategies, or at least to new ways of strategic thinking. Radically improved business processes give the business new capabilities, and therefore new strategies often emerge.

We are often asked as a part of Business Process Reengineering efforts if the team should address strategic questions. Our advice is to avoid it. It is possible, but hazardous, to run a strategy exercise in parallel with a Business Process Reengineering effort.

Business Process Reengineering efforts will always present new capabilities to the business. It is the job of the strategists to think if the capabilities should or could be exploited as core competencies in existing or new markets. Strategic thinking has replaced strategic planning.

"THE WAY BUSINESS IS CONDUCTED"

Business Process Reengineering makes the "way that business is conducted" rather than the "marketplace in which it operates" the competitive weapon of the 1990s. The Business Process Reengineering idea is to provide customer value from core business processes. So when you work within the Business Process Reengineering conceptual framework, you are always asking yourself: *How can this core business process be enhanced? How can we work in different ways that will distinguish our company, and our products, from the competition?*

Such considerations have led businesses to seek to introduce new levels of flexibility and responsiveness. This is the beginning of the holonic system and strategic thinking replacing strategic planning. The achievement of the ideas that emerge from strategic thinking is a company priority. They make the company the kind of enterprise that can thrive in both the present competitive atmosphere and in the world of the future.

To develop the vision of the competitive position of a company, strategic thinkers need to go through an exercise called scenario planning. Scenario planning is a group activity undertaken by the operational leaders of a business or across the nodes of a holonic network. In larger companies, where the strategy formulation process is an activity undertaken with dedicated staff, the strategy group joins in. The whole group gets together and brainstorms about the possible future economic, social and technical business environment.

From these brainstorm sessions, the group needs to reach a consensus about its best guess for the future. After deciding the most likely future, the group can find what core competencies the company needs to meet that future. Based on these core competencies it can then see what processes it needs to improve and exploit. Finally, it can decide what the company must look like organizationally, structurally and culturally to be most readily able to face the future.

XEROX CORPORATION

Paul Allaire is the Chairman and CEO of Xerox Corporation. When acting as a panel member at a Conference Board meeting in 1993, he addressed the audience and began with the following words.

"Our traditional sources of competitive advantage are short lived. Capital is becoming a global commodity, moving very easily across borders. Technology also is being quickly dispersed. In almost all of the markets in which we operate, we're also finding very fine skills that previously existed only in the developed countries, generally our home markets.

At the same time that these sources of competitive advantage are being less of something we can count on for the short term, our customers are also becoming substantially more demanding. In our case clearly they want to have low costs and have quality products and services, but now they also want solutions to their problems. And they want the solutions now. They are very unreasonable, very demanding of us, and require us to operate in a little different manner. We could go on and add to this complexity the demand of shareholders, employees and governments but I think it's complicated enough."

The question Allaire is asking his audience to think about is: How do you undertake strategic thinking in a useful way in this complex environment? At the Xerox Corporation they came up with an approach that captured the imagination of management and staff. This exercise, led by Allaire, provided the basis for Xerox to emerge from its competitive battles with Cannon as "The Document Company."

Allaire's view of the future, again drawing from his words at the Conference Board, is simple:

"My view of speed is that it is clearly the source of competitive advantage and, along with knowledge, is probably one of the key sources of competitive advantage for our industry for the future. What it means is you have to change all of your management processes—make them simpler, more customer focused, less bureaucratic and less centralized. And, again, have a process whereby the people closest to the action can make the decisions and implement those decisions quickly."

The next step took the Xerox Corporation from this description of the most likely future scenarios to the core competencies. In this they found the core business processes necessary to compete in that future. It involved a 12-month effort, with extensive contributions from the senior management team including Allaire.

The frame of reference for Xerox Corporation's strategic thinking was that described by Ralph D. Stacey in his book, *Managing Chaos* (Stacey, 1992). He contends that managers should begin their strategic thinking in the knowledge that the long-term future is unknowable. Therefore, a dynamic agenda of strategic issues is central to effective strategic management.

Furthermore, arising out of the currently ill-structured and conflicting issues with long-term consequences can be forged a stretching challenge that can satisfy multiple and ambiguous aspirations. This challenge can be developed by learning groups of managers, surfacing conflict, engaging in debate and publicly testing assertions.

It was clear to the Xerox Corporation team participants that they had to develop a set of capabilities and core competencies for their business to achieve competitive advantage. These capabilities and core competencies had to embody the physical characteristics of offices, locations and information technology. They also had to cover the institutional characteristics such as structure, culture and roles and the responsibilities of people. Finally, they knew they should include financial aspects such as capital investment, working capital and cash.

The strategic thinking process was conducted through a series of management workshops, with staff work being done in between to provide data. The managers began their work by determining and then voting on some 60 assumptions about the future in which they would operate.

These assumptions were set out under four headings: economy and society; organization and culture; markets and customers; and finally industry and competition.

A typical assumption under economy and society might be: "The aging of western populations will have an increased economic impact, including an impact on pensions and government spending. It will limit economic growth. Consequently, there will be a greater demand for healthcare products and pressure to raise the retirement age."

The management team then voted on the assumptions, after testing them for economic feasibility, and selected the top 20 as the scenarios for which they should prepare. For these top 20 scenarios staff work was done to develop 20 strategic imperatives. For example "Xerox must set out to actively develop the core competencies necessary to sustain competitive advantage."

These strategic imperatives enabled a small team to create the well-known strategic intent "Xerox, the document company." A longer, more measurable paragraph length explanation was also developed to clarify its meaning. "Xerox, the document company, will be the leader in the global document market and provide document services that enhance business productivity."

Next, with some staff work and workshops, the team developed 10 core competencies that it considered necessary to address the strategic imperatives. An example is, "we should develop a capability to capture and transfer knowledge."

The core competencies were then transferred to the business units and have become the basis on which all organizational change and resource investment is conducted. Xerox Corporation has decided to pursue the idea that all competitive advantage must track back to a core competence.

EXTENDING STRATEGIC THINKING TO HOLONIC RELATIONSHIPS

Each company's core business processes are part of its core competencies and are the processes it contributes to the holonic network. So it is important that they are clearly presented to potential holonic partners to understand what the company brings to the party. This is most easily done by a quickmap of the core business processes, described earlier.

Within a business unit, there is an urgent need to appoint a guardian of the quickmap, who keeps it up to date with the changing realities. Version changes to the quickmap must meet the approval of the group that did the original mapping. In a virtual company, this maintenance of the quickmap will fall to the integrator.

It is important to remember that the core business process of a holon might be a support process for the virtual company's core business process. For instance, a company with a core business process of developing and printing user manuals may join a virtual company that supplies any kind of product. It will agree to take part in the core business process of order fulfilment. By virtue of finding the node within the holonic network that is "the best" at creating, printing and storing user manuals, the virtual company will have the best value chain.

When a single company figures out which core business processes to offer to the holonic network, initially it does not need to worry about the virtual company processes. It is concerned only with defining that part of the process that it is best at. This will usually be one of its core business processes. With such processes a company can "plug and run" with other companies, divisions or business units when they come together to form a virtual company.

Spinning this logic on its head, it is apparent that within the fully formed holonic networks of the future the term "outsourcing" will really not have any meaning. Processes that are not "core" to the virtual company, which support its requirements, are handled by other nodes within the holonic network where the processes are core business processes.

The highest calibre of management process is deployed not only within each node of the virtual company, but also across the boundaries of the nodes. Strategic thinking processes that figure out which core competencies should be enhanced are needed. These strategic processes are applied, both for each individual node contributing to the virtual company and for the network as a whole.

GETTING THE RIGHT CULTURE INTO PLACE

Companies need to be ready, willing, and able to engage in a holonic network. Tom Peters describes how companies must move beyond being "learning organizations" to become "curious organizations." We define such a curious organization as one that continually adapts and adopts new, creative methods to look for BreakPoints.

In advanced societies, knowledge is the basis for almost all value. Corporations that wish to become knowledge intensive as a matter of course must invest heavily in training and electronic networks. But to become knowledge intensive as a matter of course calls for something that goes far beyond bits and bytes and hours in the classroom. Perhaps unleashing imagination is the management issue for the 1990s.

Peter Senge, writing on the learning organization, sets out some simple principles which companies can adopt in getting the right culture in place to be a holonic node. He shows how we need to be aware of the mental models that predispose our thinking and prevent learning. That we should employ systems

Table 3.1 *Characteristics of a learning organization.*

Learning approach to strategy	Internal knowledge sharing
Participative policy making	Flexible rewards
Supportive information systems	Enabling organizational structures
Supportive accounting and control	Recognition of the front line
A climate that supports personal	Learning from competitors,
development	customers
Opportunities for learning at all levels	

Source: Pedler, Burgoyne and Boydell

thinking to understand how our behaviour and attitudes are self-reinforcing. That therefore a quick fix will not work unless we think through all the steps necessary to reinforce the behaviour and attitudes that are necessary to make it work. He describes how to change we need to be self-aware and we need personal mastery to consciously change our attitudes and behaviour and to show it to others. He then describes how shared vision is necessary for shared learning and thus the importance of the strategic thinking process (just as we have described earlier in this chapter). Finally, he proves that team learning will go further than individual learning. The process is more creative and it enables us to recognize and overcome patterns of defensive behavior that undermine our performance.

Pedler, Burgoyne and Boydell in their consulting practice have developed 11 practical insights into the characteristics of a learning organization. We list these in Table 3.1 as a helpful checklist for those seeking to be a holonic node. These are in practice best evaluated using their full 55 question research method.

In our work with companies undertaking a Business Process Reengineering program we often find it useful to explore these issues through the simple questionnaire given in Table 3.2. This was first developed for publication in *International Management* magazine by Patrick McHugh. We have modified it to help you learn if you are likely to be a good holonic node.

The culture of the organization must be that it is all right to make mistakes. This means a capability to change gear in the middle of things and to drop old processes and products in exchange for new or even experimental efforts.

Part of this culture is the discovery of what we call the "new" assets. These are the people, brands and image, process technology, knowledge, information, distribution and supply

Table 3.2 Questionnaire. *The following self-assessment questions devised by consultants Coopers & Lybrand detects whether a company is ready to make a success of Business Process Reengineering. Each requires a simple yes or no (Y/N) answer.*

1   Do you review customer perception of your products and services monthly? Y/N
2   Does the team's reward depend specifically on achieving some measure of customer satisfaction? Y/N
3   Can you define your company's basis of competition as a process based core competence? Y/N
4   Have you benchmarked your company's core business processes against those of your major competitors? Y/N
5   Does your business use process costing? Y/N
6   Could you write down more than three non-financial quantified targets for your company? Y/N
7   Has a new technology caused a major shift in your company's activity during the past three years? Y/N
8   Do you have a unique technical competitive advantage in any of your core business processes? Y/N
9   Is your company vulnerable to a take over? Y/N
10 For new investments in core business processes do you have a return-on-capital expenditure hurdle of at least 20%? Y/N
11 For new investments in non-core business processes do you have a return-on-capital expenditure hurdle of at least 50 percent? Y/N
12 Does the head of your company pursue personal recognition ahead of recognition of your business? Y/N
13 Does the head of your company emphasize how people are expected to act? Y/N
14 Is there a commonly held view of the likely market share that will be held by your company in five years' time? Y/N
15 Have you any business process or cross-functionally oriented teams? Y/N
16 Do you consider that teams are less successful at achieving their goals than individuals? Y/N
17 Was the last major reorganization in your company more than one year ago? Y/N
18 Has your company ever launched a new product or service that if it failed would destroy the company? Y/N
19 Is it difficult for individuals to make career moves between different functions in the company? Y/N
20 Is everyone in the company required to undertake more than five days' training each year? Y/N
21 Are you achieving a 20 per cent or more annual effectiveness improvement in your core business processes? Y/N

Assessment
Score 1 for each answer that tallies with the following:
1Y; 2Y; 3Y; 4Y; 5Y; 6Y; 7Y; 8Y; 9N; 10N; 11Y; 12Y;
13Y; 14Y; 15Y; 16N; 17N; 18Y; 19N; 20Y; 21Y.

Table 3.2 *Continued*

Interpretation

Score 0–7
You have a long way to go. So many conditions for success are absent that the scale of the change needed will be beyond your current capability. Instead you should undertake targeted improvement programs in a few areas such as customer research, market share projections and cross-functional teams.

Score 8–14
You have got some conditions—begin to think about how a reengineering program could make a significant difference.

Score 15–21
You have great potential as a holonic node. You need to reorient your strategic thinking around participation in holonic networks.

relationships that create value. They are the hallmark of the twenty-first century company and of the virtual company. The virtual company is made up of many nodes. In virtual companies process-based capabilities such as the "new" assets will take precedence over product-based capabilities.

In our book *Business Process Reengineering* (Johansson *et al.*, 1993), we describe at length the "new" assets and the role they play in company programs. In the last few years, since we wrote the book, things have changed a little. We have begun to consult with businesses that are thinking along holonic lines. Their strategic thinking in particular has included the use of the "new" assets as capabilities and sometimes core competencies.

We have added two new, "new" assets which are concerned with knowledge, personal relationships and professional expertise. These can be extended to the management of suppliers, distribution networks and even customers. We call these supply equity and distribution equity. Such knowledge is critical in the formation of virtual companies in a holonic network.

One company has put many of the ideas in this chapter to work and come out a winner. Their holonic network shows how both large and small companies can compete using virtual companies and thus go beyond Business Process Reengineering.

APRILIA—A VISION OF FLEXIBILITY

Aprilia, the Italian manufacturer of motorcycles and scooters, is a leading industrial company in creating a holonic network. In 1993, the 430 person company had revenues of about $220 million and was the third largest manufacturer of cycles and scooters in Europe. Revenues doubled from 1990 to 1993, and volumes increased 128 percent.

By focusing on core business processes, an unremitting Total Quality effort, and using the principles of "co-makership" with its component manufacturers, Aprilia has created a company in which time-to-market for new models is 12 months (half the time of its nearest competitors), with quality levels as good as top Japanese producers, and top machine performance (as demonstrated by winning some of the World Championship motorcycle titles).

The company has been chosen by BMW to build its new motorcycle model because of its World Championship performances. Where once Italian motorcycle manufacturers were unable to compete with the Japanese, today Aprilia is taking market share from Japanese manufacturers throughout Europe.

Aprilia took the remains of some Italian companies that were failing against Japanese competition in the 1970s and 1980s. They combined the capabilities and core competencies from all of the former companies to grow Aprilia from scratch, based on the idea of a company that would be an integrator, designing motor cycles then finding component manufacturers and stimulating those component manufacturers to come up with creative solutions. By defining its strategic direction as an integrator, it was important the company collect as much understanding of process technology as possible.

Aprilia's business processes are largely decentralized, with many support processes and much manufacturing outsourced. Over 100 employees (about 25 percent of the workforce) are engineers. Revenue per employee in fiscal 1994 was $511 000, nearly twice that of other major European cycle manufacturers. Some Aprilia engineers are stationed at either the OEM site or at suppliers' sites to make sure of continuity throughout the value chain.

The company has grown rapidly because of its business systems, which leverage the work of its employees (its engineering team creates as much output as teams three times as large) while reducing the company's need for investment by largely purchasing components from other nodes (only final assembly is done by Aprilia workers).

Aprilia has a network of about 250 suppliers, about 20 of whom are considered key suppliers, or "partners." However they limit the work they do for Aprilia to a maximum of 30 percent of the partner's production volume. This allows the partners to reduce their risk should Aprilia's business fall off. It also affords them the opportunity to add capabilities and build core competencies by working for other companies (a situation Aprilia actively endorses).

The pool of suppliers ranges from quite small companies to global giants. In the geographic area around Aprilia's plants, the company has helped to nurture and develop the skill base of several small companies with no prior experience in the motorcycle industry. Most of the company's suppliers of technological components are not located in the same geographic areas.

Aprilia has created a network of suppliers with a high degree of flexibility. The network is able to manage volume flexibility of from 2000 to 18 000 pieces per month. This is due to a rapidly changing product mix (scooters have a short selling season, only in the spring and summer).

All of Aprilia's suppliers share the same values when working with Aprilia in its holonic network. These include a small local machine shop and the giant Bombardier Group of Canada. Bombardier has annual revenues of $4.7 billion and supplies engines made by its Rotax company to Aprilia.

They have a very high level of mutual trust. The largest suppliers, like Rotax and Minarelli, participate in new product development, agreeing to new engine specifications without any guarantee or formal contract. Simultaneously, Aprilia shows its commitment to smaller, local companies by speaking to these companies' bankers and helping them to secure loans to gear up production.

All of the participating companies agree to come into each virtual company as a business decision, there is not pressure to "play now or not play later." They may even agree to participate

Figure 3.3   *Aprilia's holonic network for motorcycle design and manufacturing*

in only some production for a particular product. This kind of autonomy and distributed entrepreneurial capability is far different from the Japanese *Kieretsu* system. Under this system suppliers are captive to the OEM at the top of the pyramid, and are told if, when and how much they will produce. It is also quite different from the way Benetton—often held as the model of Italian business networking—operates; Benetton owns many of its upstream manufacturers.

In the Aprilia network, information circulates quickly. During new product development, the system is completely inter-communicating. Suppliers of engines and other major components can work in parallel as there is a high degree of information transparency. The core business process for each opportunity establishes itself as the most able businesses offer to join in. The operational processes are not as tightly connected through EDI as the design processes, but Aprilia is actively working on improving that aspect of the virtual company.

Within the network, many participants function as more than one type of node. Aprilia's engineering unit is a resource node of motorcycle knowledge, and an integrator node which uses the knowledge and capabilities of the system. The network also has operational nodes such as those that do final assembly and sell the product.

Rotax and Minarelli, the engine suppliers, are both knowledge resource and operational nodes possessing a great knowledge of engines which they manufacture for the network.

Other suppliers also act as operational nodes, providing components and subassemblies.

Many of Aprilia's suppliers are also suppliers to the other large Italian motorcycle company, Cagivi-Ducati, which takes advantage of the products and processes developed by these suppliers to satisfy Aprilia. But it too adds to the suppliers' capabilities.

Aprilia, Cagivi-Ducati and increasingly BMW, which has asked Aprilia to design and manufacture its 650 cc engined motorcycles, are creating a large holonic network. The network includes Minarelli, Rotax (Bombardier) and a host of smaller suppliers throughout the Venice area and also in Emilia-Romangna, and Lombardy in Italy, Linz in Austria, and Munich and Berlin in Germany. The network is illustrated in Figure 3.3.

4
The Dynamics of the System

It should be clear by now that the ideas of Business Process Reengineering are made more valuable by the creation of a holonic network. Business Process Reengineering provides a comprehensive operational response to the strategic thinking of the holonic network's initiators. This is because the ideas of Business Process Reengineering provide two mechanisms for progress. First, each holon can progress individually by focusing ever more closely on its core business process. Second, the network as a whole can optimize its virtual companies' core business processes.

Robert Hayes and Stephen Wheelwright (1984) in *Restoring our Competitive Edge: Competing through Manufacturing*, suggested that a mechanism for growth would be to apply a business's core competence in manufacturing to new product areas. Thus, the Archer Division of RJR Nabisco, once it had reduced the changeover time for equipment from 36 hours to a little more than one hour was able to enter new markets. The Archer Division manufactures cigarette boxes and packages including the foil. When it was able to make printed foils of different types and colors in smaller production runs it could sell its foil in other applications such as packaging for peanuts, Alka-Seltzer and Sanka coffee as well as florist foil.

The key idea behind Business Process Reengineering is that there are only a few core business processes in which BreakPoints can be found. Within a holonic network, once the BreakPoint is identified, companies in the network can focus their improvement efforts on a common target. Attention to core business processes that touch the customer, rather than attention to functions, keeps old organizational barriers and handoffs from interfering with the Business Process Reengineering effort. For example, 3M has as its core competence the ability to spread something onto a substrate, cut it up and package it. Everything from sandpaper to cellophane tape and magnetic tape to Post-it notes uses this core competence.

Core business processes after a reengineering effort should function without capacity limitation. This enables a business that has moved beyond Business Process Reengineering and joined a holonic network to enter virtual companies with ease. The business no longer need be concerned by rigidly structured core and support business processes. Often the business will have stripped itself back to only its core competencies to achieve this level of flexibility.

The idea of operating a core business process without capacity limitation may seem contradictory with the idea of cost savings through Business Process Reengineering. However, it is not. First, whenever a company reengineers a core business process there is, by definition, excess capacity (otherwise you would not have any savings). In businesses where we have worked we have found as much as 50 percent excess capacity, even in process and capital-intensive industries. Furthermore, a company can afford excess capacity in its core processes since it is trading off the cost of support and management processes. Excess capacity is in fact necessary. That is what the company uses as leverage in the marketplace.

At first blush, a company stripped to only its core competencies may have difficulty gaining credibility with the banks and the stock market, as bankers and money managers ask how the company can operate. However, since these institutions value a business primarily by its return on assets, they should soon be convinced of the value in pure competence-based businesses. In fact the return on assets and equity of a business acting as a holon are considerably improved and increased revenue should have increased profitability.

There are a host of new ways in which the financial community should look at companies acting as holons to convince themselves of the value of such an operating style. First, they should consider the value of any proprietary technology. Second, they should consider the "new" assets and value these in the way that many are now considering brands.

Third, they need to evaluate the impact of the business's ownership or participation in knowledge networks that understand and respond to the market better than the competition. Fourth, by more completely using core process capital investment and outsourcing support and management processes, a company's financial use of total capital employed—sometimes called the economic value added (EVA)—will be vastly improved.

Finally, the business must be considered more stable. It has increased strength through its participation with other holonic nodes. All holonic nodes have a mutual interest in a network's complete success.

To reengineer core and support business processes in a holon and in a holonic network requires the node to have many capabilities. How these capabilities, such as an ability to learn and to use knowledge effectively, are developed is described later in this chapter.

ORGANIC SYSTEMS IN BUSINESS

Traditional approaches to business performance improvement have applied "mechanical" logic. This improves performance "company by company," using mass-production-oriented functions. In looking beyond Business Process Reengineering, we sought to understand what might happen using "organic" logic, which would be more flexible and market oriented. The result of this was the discovery of the holonic organic system.

Organic systems have vitality, structure and purpose. They are able to adapt and react to external stimuli. There are thousands of organic models in nature and we know that they provide many analogies for business. We found the holonic system in nature and by studying it we discovered that it is directly applicable to business. We believe that in the future more ideas for business systems will be found in nature than in the minds of theorists and business school academics. The idea of applying the holonic system to business might seem futuristic, however it is currently being applied. As usual the entrepreneurial urge has evolved faster than the observer's curiosity. One could argue that sating the observer's curiosity leads to entrepreneurship.

Holonic networks exhibit organic characteristics in that they are continually evolving through interaction with the environment. Most large companies today would argue that they too are continually evolving with the marketplace. However, the degree of flexibility and speed of response that is present in holonic networks are an order of magnitude greater. The evolution is more rapid in a holonic network, which can pick up or drop nodes. A large organization purchases new process capabilities or hires new people. Large organizations are also inherently slow at removing old capabilities, due to labor laws and union action.

The holonic network is also more flexible than a single company. It is able to move to new market positions without feeling that it needs to protect its old position. Finally, the holonic network has greater capacity flexibility. It can take on new partners, with their available capacity, more readily than the large company can find or lay down new capital equipment.

In a holonic system in nature there is an ontogenic aspect, in that each holon has some process capability excellence and survives by dint of that excellence. There is also a phylogenic aspect; the holonic system survives because the combination of the unique process capabilities of the holons is more powerful and flexible than that of the individual members alone.

In Chapter 1 we discussed how the Portuguese man-of-war was a model for the holonic business system. The Portuguese man-of-war is a distant cousin of the jellyfish. It got its name because it looks like an old Portuguese warship. A man-of-war is really a colony of hundreds of animals, called hydrozoans, joined under a sort of balloon that keeps them afloat. The tentacles can be several meters long. They trail through the water as the main float is blown along by the wind. The man-of-war's tentacles carry very painful and dangerous stings (Figure 4.1).

Each hydrozoan in the colony we call a holon. Each holon has its own job. Some catch food and others digest it. The Portuguese

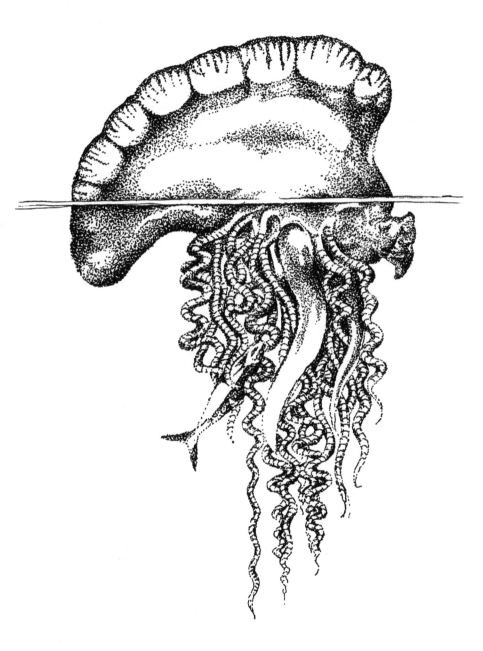

Figure 4.1   Portuguese man-of-war. (Approximately a third actual size)

man-of-war communicates between its various holons through the "blood" supply and nervous system as holons react to external events. Each animal is born into the creature and lives its life within its structure and rules. No one knows the age of a Portuguese man-of-war.

In a similar way, companies join and leave a holonic network. Just as the holons adapt to their individual tasks in the Portuguese man-of-war, so too do the companies in a holonic network.

More than one holon exists for each task in the Portuguese man-of-war, and although they compete with each other holons are dependent upon each other's success. So too are holons dependent upon each other in a commercial holonic network. Holons may have similar capabilities and compete with each other, yet their success is bound into the success of the network.

A holonic network in the commercial world is a group of businesses that, acting in an integrated and organic manner, is able to configure itself to manage each business opportunity that its customers present. The Portuguese man-of-war can configure its holons to deal with each new fish trapped in its tentacles.

Physical characteristics in a commercial holonic network are as easily visible as those of the Portuguese man-of-war. First, the network is not an individual business or a single animal. Second, it has an autonomous distributed management hierarchy, and therefore no apparent single leader. Third, the commercial holonic network has an autonomous distributed information system.

The holonic network, by definition, is process based and lives by business process logic. The Portuguese man-of-war reacts to the capture of a fish or to the strength of the wind, and not to the activity of a single holon. The analogy for commercial holonic networks is that managers have to learn to manage by processes and not by functions. The holonic network distributes management processes among its participating holons. Not only is there no hierarchy and only minimal management overhead in the holonic network, but this is mirrored in each holon.

There are signs that some company acquisitions made today exploit the process and management capabilities of companies and fit them to serve as holons in holonic networks. The acquiring business strips management overhead from the company and leaves the process to manage itself. The difference in style from traditional businesses that results from such changes in ownership is apparent in the holonic network and the virtual companies that form within it. A Japanese company, Koa, buys process capability, strips out the management overhead and leaves the workers to manage themselves. Operators take responsibility for the activities that occur in the businesses and undertake management processes where necessary.

The company Leitz was heavily in debt to the banks before it was acquired by Wild, to form Wild Leitz, a German camera and instrument manufacturer. Later Wild Leitz merged with Cambridge Instruments. The merger with Wild Leitz effectively took Cambridge Instruments out of the stock market. Cambridge Instruments merged with a company approximately three times bigger than itself. The 40/60 merger was possible because its balance sheet was significantly better than Wild's. Cambridge Instruments had only 11 percent bank loans out of its total shareholder equity.

Wild Leitz effectively acquired Cambridge Instruments for its management capability. After the acquisition the new group, which took the name of the famous camera, Leica, had far fewer managers in the combined companies than before. The Group, now based in Switzerland, has a small corporate management of about 30 people. The new Group acts in a holonic way in the product development process. Here it establishes a virtual company from its subsidiaries for each new development based on their technical core competence.

INFORMATION TECHNOLOGY IN THE HOLONIC NETWORK

In many early Business Process Reengineering efforts it was difficult to distinguish the activities undertaken in the name of Business Process Reengineering from systems' implementation programs. This was due to the origins of many early Business Process Reengineering enthusiasts. Information technology was regarded as "the enabler" for Business Process Reengineering. Reengineering efforts were launched to prepare the ground for more effective information systems' implementation. The supporters of information-technology-based Business Process Reengineering often take one view; namely that the "system is the solution." However, it simply is not good enough to spend money on new technology and then to use it in the same old way.

We are happy to support any effort that will result in improved business performance. However, we have found the Harvard economist Gary Loveman's words, which he spoke to a conference of computer executives in 1991, to ring true: "I'm here to tell you that after several years my results have been poor. Poor in the sense that [I] simply cannot find evidence that there has been a substantial productivity increase—and in some cases any productivity increases—from the substantial growth in information technology."

We have seen some examples of information technology that rebut these views. We have seen on-line retrieval and rapid distribution of information provide performance enhancements in some areas. Examples are in data-intensive activities such as reservation and banking systems, and in complex data-intensive design projects. Several speakers at conferences have reported that after many years of decline, white collar productivity is showing some upturn because of information technology.

However, the overemphasis on information technology in Business Process Reengineering has had two negative effects. First, it has caused many senior managers to delegate the reengineering effort to their information systems department. Because of this it has been denied the central role in operational performance improvement that it should occupy. Second, reengineering has become a tool for computer systems implementation. Only, in two fields, "drug abuse" and "information technology," are people routinely called "users." It seems that the computer is often used as an enormous storage bin that spits out, on command, obsolete data for the major purpose of self-justification of the user.

In our previous book (Johansson *et al.*, 1993) we took the view that the provision of information technology and the "new" asset, information, should be treated as support processes for the core business processes. As companies move beyond Business Process Reengineering and toward the holonic enterprise, we realize that the holonic business system requires each holon to make common and substantial use of a computer network. The holonic network is therefore the first business system that is truly dependent on computing for its operation.

For the virtual company and holonic network to function correctly, it is essential that information gets through to a wide range of individuals. Each individual needs as a minimum to have access to all the information that he or she needs. This may be required to develop an idea or to carry out the tasks allocated by the network.

In order to explore new ideas, individuals also need to be able to obtain any other information on the holon or the network. Even if this information is not used, the right to access it shows the degree of trust placed in all individuals in the holonic network. In holonic networks information is a "new" asset that is freely available to all. Access and exchange of information is also freely accomplished from outside the network.

For example, when concurrent engineering takes place across many nodes, as it does in the holonic networks set up to serve the automotive OEMs, the design effort is managed so that concept-to-market time is some 50–60 percent less than before. This is hard enough to achieve within the individual company, but the coordination effort required grows as a factorial when information must flow across many nodes. The virtual company must use work flow software and I/O queue control to manage its effort. Also, designs must be available simultaneously at any point in the network for simulation and interference calculations. The network cannot afford to design a vehicle like the Camero, which initially had to have its engine block pulled to extract the sparkplugs!

The purpose of the computer in holonic networks is for immediate distribution of data. People can instantaneously use it to make "gut feel" decisions that affect the continued excellence of the holonic network. Implicit in the idea of distributing data to people in the holonic network is the notion of a single node that manages the information system. This presents a few problems for nodes that participate in several holonic networks. However, open system and open communications architectures, exemplified by OSI and the Internet, have overcome these difficulties.

There are many information types present in holonic networks. A list of just some of them shows how complex the communication and information provision task can be.

For example, design information needs to reach all parts of the holonic network. The starting point for service information required by field engineers is design information. When a potential order enters the holonic network, it circulates rapidly to enable holons to "bid" for their part in the contract. The integrator will search the holons for design innovations and core capabilities. After a contract award, product configuration information must be collected to enable billing and later servicing to take place.

Invariably, continuous improvement relies on the existence of an activity-based costing system. Manufacturing holons and sales outlets need accurate demand information. The consumer drives the materials' management system through the demand-driven logistics ideas described in Chapter 5. All of these activities are enabled by information technology.

Transportation information, quality information, feedback loops, maintenance information, customer tracking information, and green information together create not just an information network, but a knowledge network. But it takes more than just information technology for this knowledge network to emerge; it takes the actions of the people in the holonic network.

MANAGEMENT STYLE IN A HOLONIC NETWORK

The holonic network, and the virtual companies that form within it, are innately entrepreneurial. There are four types of nodes in a holonic system, "resource" nodes, "support" nodes, "integrator" nodes and "operational" nodes. No matter the type of node the management style necessary to operate a node within a holonic network is the entrepreneurial style.

Top managers of nodes have a high degree of creativity and flexibility, and they work by priority. Entrepreneurial management drives for effectiveness, rather than merely for efficiency. Entrepreneurial managers are willing to take risks. They make decisions quickly based on a "gut feel" for the situation, rather than by analyzing each decision in agonizing detail. They realize there is no such thing as "perfect information," and that waiting for and hoping that perfect information will develop only leads to indecision and stagnation. "Gut feel" does not develop on its own. It is the result of years of experience both within each node and within the wider business environment.

When pressed, successful CEOs invariably admit that they make their decisions by "gut feel." Life in a node within a holonic network requires that some but not all decisions should be pushed down the line to the individuals most capable of making the decisions. A holonic network requires a great deal of flexibility. There is not the time to scrub the numbers and move them up the line for decision making.

This style of working is uncomfortable for some CEOs, who fear a loss of control. But as "Red" Petersen, the CEO who turned Ford toward the holonic style of operation, said: "It is tough for a boss to tell his subordinates that they know more about something than he does and to run with their instincts on something. He has to have the self-confidence to trust and empower people below him in the company hierarchy."

Most managers consider work done by outsiders as inferior and would prefer to keep as much as possible under their own control. For example, customer-specific tests on integrated circuits such as those manufactured for the fictional MEGA-PC are usually unnecessary and add significantly to cost. Yet there continues to be a lack of trust of integrated circuit manufacturers.

This lack of trust, and a perception that control is best achieved by oneself, detracts from a concentration on core business processes and adds overhead. As Richard Marcus, former CEO of Neiman Marcus said in *Business Week:* "In the past, if something was worth doing, you did it yourself. But, there is just not enough time in the day to manage everything."

Many customers insist upon knowing their order status at each supplier, yet more often than not delivery reliability is a contractual requirement. There is a direct relationship between the number of order status inquiries and the amount of excess inventory at the customer's site.

AT&T in Little Rock made PCs and keyboards; yet the business unit insisted on making 720 different screws to "have control over the process." This is more than just stubbornness; the keyboards were disposable and should never have been fastened with screws in the first place.

Many companies are making strides in their trust of outsiders. Witness the receiving dock where inspection no longer takes place for many items. Great, you say. But there is still a receiving dock, because the parts are still counted and logged in. Consider how much money is spent auditing a supplier's competency when, in reality, the supplier knows considerably more about his product and its controls than the auditor.

The style of management within the holonic network exhibits itself in many dimensions that contrast vividly with more traditional styles. Among these dimensions are management by strategic thinking, described in Chapter 3. Managers also exercise their power through teams and a network of contacts rather than through a hierarchy.

Teams reject strongly an autocratic style and are in favor of a more persuasive, advocacy and coaching style of leadership. For example, in an autocratic workplace, the consequences of a poor decision must be explained. But if a person properly empowered makes a wrong decision then there can be no retribution. If blame were to be attributed, it would undermine the basis of the holonic network. Surely not every decision made will be right. But, to paraphrase the American basketball star Michael Jordan, it is better to make a decision that turns out to be wrong than not to make a decision because you are afraid to. Many people felt Jordan made a bad decision coming out of retirement after a career in basketball to try to play professional baseball.

In a holonic network the process sets the organization's structure. In a holon the classical tree diagram for organizational structure is turned upside down. It looks like an inverted pyramid. In a holonic network the managers are at the service of the network and the network at the service of the individual in the holons. In the end, however, everyone is at the service of the final customer.

In a holonic network, virtual companies within the network, and the nodes that make up the virtual companies, a new type of relationship emerges between companies, the management and the workforce. Cooperation and mutual trust become the watchwords. Management by process rather than by function is demanding and requires highly flexible and agile management processes and systems.

For instance, Chrysler has been given much credit for leading the way into the holonic model within the US automotive industry. All of the reasons for embarking on the holonic pathway were present—the need to develop agile suppliers, the high cost of innovation, design and capital equipment, and the need to keep up with the speed of technology development. *Fortune* magazine also notes that the correct cultural ingredients were present at Chrysler: flexibility of management, absence of institutional barriers, strong leadership and urgency of mission.

MAINTAINING CAPABILITIES BY LEARNING

Management by process rather than by function also requires new skills, including the leadership of activities by capability and the leadership of core processes by core competence. The maintenance of capability is the central role for managers in a holonic node, which must always provide the most effective core business process and continually improve the efficiency of its operations—or change them—to meet each prosumer's needs.

Thus the node needs as one of its capabilities the ability to learn. There are several ways to develop this capability, including transferring people around the network, creating knowledge networks and appointing knowledge managers.

By working alongside people with different skills and moving around the network as each virtual company requires, individuals are able to impart knowledge obtained by previous experience. In this way the holonic network taps maximum expertise potential and ensures that the process of ongoing improvement becomes a matter of course. Thus although the holonic network is not self-learning—although it is self-improving and self-differentiating—each node is self-learning, and its capability adds to the network's capabilities.

We have already referred to knowledge networks as they relate to information technology. Knowledge networks have many characteristics that distinguish them from traditional systems networks. First, they can be used to obtain knowledge rather than simply information or data. Second, they contain data from many sources external to the organization. Third, they are maintained by a system and people who capture and structure information for later operational application.

At the risk of seeming self-serving, we consider management consulting to be a good example of a holonic network in action today. Each client engagement is unique and prosumer driven. It requires the configuration of a new virtual company with a unique balance of skill sets. The assignment can be local, national or global. The need for up-to-date data and experience is critical to meeting the prosumer's needs and desires.

A good example of a knowledge network has been set up in Coopers & Lybrand's offices to support Business Process Reengineering services. Data is captured by two full-time professional staff and entered into the system. This data includes experience statements from completed and running jobs. It also includes published articles, market research data, experience with the use of different techniques and internal and external reports. The network is available by modem from any telephone in the world. Search programs enable the person logged into the knowledge network to make connections between key words in documents and to trace relationships. All management consultants using the knowledge network are required to contribute information.

No knowledge network will operate without people whose task it is to build and maintain the knowledge network. At McKinsey & Co., a management consulting firm, a partner is assigned for some weeks by rotation to run the knowledge network. His or her task is to find the latest data and assignment experience and to make it available to others in the worldwide McKinsey business who may need it. An added incentive is given to people to contribute to the knowledge network through their annual appraisal. Each consultant is judged to some extent on the value that he or she has added to himself or herself and to the company—through the network and through individual assignments—over the last year.

NODES REFLECT NETWORK CHARACTERISTICS

Holonic networks require similar characteristics from their nodes, and each node must display the same characteristics for inclusion in the network. Thus over time it becomes apparent that each node adopts the characteristics of the entire network. These characteristics are that the node is non-hierarchical, time based, value driven and ecologically-harmonic, as discussed in Chapter 1.

All members adopt the same operational philosophy. In 1985, Coopers & Lybrand undertook a survey that among others questions asked why a company was carrying out JIT. Almost three out of four of those who were carrying out JIT said their "suppliers could supply them in a JIT mode" and that they "could not take full advantage of their supplier's capability." Around the same time, a study published in the *Journal of Purchasing and Materials Management*, showed that 85 percent of the sample interviewed had carried out JIT, against only 39 percent of their first tier suppliers. These contradictory results tell us that, clearly, companies were not all on the same wavelength about what Just-in-Time is, and may account for some dissatisfaction with Just-in-Time efforts; when all was said and done nearly all did not cross company boundaries to affect the value chain.

If JIT or any other philosophy is to be the one of choice in the holonic network, then each node must subscribe to and carry out that approach. Or else, they may apply their own alternative philosophy so that it satisfies the network's requirements. These requirements include speed and quality. Any alternative philosophy must be totally transparent to the network participants and must integrate operationally with the network.

REGULATION OF HOLONIC NETWORKS

A holonic network is self-regulating and in dynamic equilibrium. Demand-driven logistics manage the entire capacity chain through capacity pull signals sent by the asset manager. Negative feedback is the backbone of demand-driven logistics that manages the "sequential" flow of value added through the manufacturing process. By definition these pull signals are self-regulating, since they operate on the principle of negative feedback. This principle says that output of "something" controls the rate at which the "something" produces the output. More simply, the holonic network only produces something when there is an external demand for the item.

Through the regulation of capacity—and indirectly capability—the entire holonic network is self-regulating. New capacity is added to a node only when demand requires it and capacity is removed as demand declines. A holonic network can therefore be said to be in dynamic equilibrium.

The detailed mechanisms of self-regulation rely on communal decision-making processes. In a self-regulating system the leaders of the holonic network come together to establish the rules of operation. These rules are extensive and comprehensive so that circumstances can, as far as possible, be anticipated. The rules deal with many matters including the resolution of disputes and the addition or removal of a node from the network. The rules also set out the knowledge network and design standards. They describe in addition the appointment procedure for nodes joining a virtual company, and the allocation of profits to each holon participating in a virtual company.

In the book, *Organizations in Action*, J. D. Thompson (1967) describes three types of relationships that can exist between parts of an organization. First, they may be sequential in a traditional value chain, that is A ships to B who ships to C. Second, they may be pooled, that is different parts or entities each contribute to form a whole. Third, they may be reciprocal. In the reciprocal relationship the output of each entity becomes the input to the entity from which they get their own input. Holonic networks and virtual companies are different from these traditional types of relationships in that they exhibit both pooled and reciprocal type characteristics.

Richard Normann and Rafael Ramírez (1994) in the book, *Designing Interactive Strategy: Value Chain to Value Constellation*, use the notion of reciprocal type relationships to expand their thesis that suppliers must "get and give" constant reactions from and to their customers. Their simple example is the auto dealer who gives constant responses to the automotive OEM. In this way the OEM can further improve the physical design or characteristics of the car. The OEM can also provide dealer packages that make the car more desirable to the car buyer. This aspect of customer "get and give," results in an improved market offering from a holonic network. Each node exploits its core competence, and collectively they apply their capabilities to product improvement.

The regulation of complex business systems is a difficult task since there are many independent and interdependent variables that must be controlled. Various approaches to the management of complex systems have emerged in recent years.

CONSISTENCY

The issue of consistency concerns turning strategic imperatives into short-term decisions. Short-term decisions that are consistent with strategic thinking are a hallmark of holonic nodes. For example, there are many ways to reduce manufacturing costs. You can purchase ever more standardized parts, becoming more of an assembly operation. You can automate, if this will truly reduce total costs, not just labor costs. You can seek by design to include ever more of the product's functions in software. You can avoid options and inventory by making to order rather than to stock. You can shorten manufacturing process times, again with an impact on inventory.

A consistent company approach forces management decisions regarding the short term to conform to the strategic imperatives. These include how it will buy, sell, manufacture and deliver goods and services.

ATTAINING THE COMPETENCE FOR NETWORK PARTICIPATION

Holonic networks have many prerequisites. First, nodes must have some shared vision of their role and the place of the holonic network in the business environment. To overcome operational difficulties holonic networks have also to decide the "game rules." More than "game rules," however, there has to be trust between nodes. Participants in the holonic network should center this trust on a flexible, interactive and open relationship. We have observed that such trust can be built on unilateral actions taken by a node. For example, a node may declare that it will from now on source all its components from another network participant, or it may decide unilaterally to outsource a previously performed function.

The most important element of trust concerns the market's and the node's relationship with customers. This means that each node should potentially have an open prosumer channel to the market. Through this channel the network can exercise its core competencies. Nonetheless, to communicate rapidly the information from the prosumers to the nodes, it is necessary to have a "real-time" shared information system. Also the network must have a critical level of presence through its nodes in the territory that concerns the prosumer. Establishing such real-time contact with prosumers again requires significant effort.

We have seen businesses move people into the offices of their customers and send sales staff on technical training courses to develop this closeness. Mayakawa, a Japanese manufacturer of specialty ovens, supplies an engineer to every major customer. That engineer intimately knows all the customer's requirements and future needs—sometimes before the customer does. In this way, Mayakawa can anticipate new technology or refinements in the customer's industry, and be ready to service quickly that customer's unique requirements.

The virtual company hinges on group working. Individuals have increased personal skills. Many products of the virtual company require interdisciplinary skills to design, manufacture, deliver and service. Many people thus apply their expertise in different combinations, according to the particular virtual company in which they are employed. Information technology enables such specialist teams at many thousands of miles distance from each other to work together.

We have observed that team working requires careful introduction. Such an introduction includes education and training in the techniques of team management. It also requires individuals to assess their own approach to team working. Finally, it requires time to experiment and to learn that team working is both more enjoyable and more effective than individual initiative.

In Asea Brown Boveri's Power Plant Controls (ABB-PPC)— one of ABB's 50-odd international business areas—team working is the basis on which the holonic network operates. In this business, which designs and installs controls for electrical power generating plants, new orders can enter from anywhere in the world. The business area, however, has design groups in three countries.

Issues the company must deal with are, first, how to get the best from each of these design teams into the final specification and second, how to make the design as responsive as possible to local needs. ABB-PPC has tackled this by creating a worldwide computer network that enables designers to communicate at all times. It has also invested in extensive travel and education so that the people around the world know each other and their capabilities. Finally, ABB-PPC operates a policy of transfers between design groups and installation teams that ensures that all designers are familiar with "best practices."

It is important for the leader of each node to establish the correct relationship with the team members under his charge. His behavior will be taken by the team members as the model for their behavior, and they will emulate him. The leader must be open and honest with the team so that the team members trust him and each other. It is advisable for the leader to describe his management style and to invite questions on it. In this way team members do not imagine him weak or unsure of himself. The team leader must be clear about his own willingness to invest time in developing his team to quality long-term relationships and performance. If the leader only pays lip service to team building he will get no more than he pays for. Dedication to the team-building process in a holon pays off.

Every node must fully understand the prosumer's needs, requirements and wishes. The nodes also have to decide what they can do to complement the core business process for each customer. Therefore, at the initiation of a new virtual company, each node must undertake both "routing by walking around" and "quality function deployment" exercises to see how the customer uses the product. These ideas are well accepted in purchasing management, and are known as the Co-Op methodology, discussed in more detail in Chapter 5. The question is what can the node do to help the prosumer. In its way each node adds value to the product. This is "synergy of value".

The Co-Op methodology is a powerful tool for increasing performance and trust. At a shoe manufacturing company in Leicester, England, the first operation in preparing the soles was to reach into an enormous box and sort the rights from the lefts. Yet, the press that punches the sole always works in pairs. When the customer walked round the plant he asked "Why take the right sole from the press with the right hand and the left sole with the left hand and throw them into a common box?" He had noticed not only that the box was twice as cumbersome to handle, but also that precious time was wasted sorting 250 pairs of soles.

CTB works constantly with teachers so that the company can, through the norm-referenced tests, tell them something that they do not know about individual pupils. Ultimately of course the pupil is the teacher's customer. With this feedback teachers can further help their pupils.

In our previous book (Johansson *et al.*, 1993) we referred to an engineer's need for safe design, and how one transformer company offered a step-higher rated transformer at the same price as the lower specification. The justification for redesigning and retooling the entire product line came when the company realized that it had a BreakPoint after significant interaction with many customers. The engineers in these customers also had a paramount desire for safety and so opted for the company's higher safety rated transformers whenever they had a choice. The company was also able to significantly rationalize its product offerings.

5
The Mechanics of the System

It is all right for businesses that ally themselves in a holonic network to share values. It is fine to believe that by acting together they are more able to compete than if they acted alone. But in order for a holonic network to be a commercial success, products and services must be economically delivered to customers.

We call the system that ensures economic delivery of physical products demand-driven logistics.* It is the backbone of the actual day-to-day execution of a virtual company. By forming a virtual company among and integrating with a product's suppliers, the end customer can be more completely serviced. In return this rewards suppliers with increased orders and market share.

But even before a virtual company can be created, the relationship between each "customer" and each "supplier" within a holonic network must be created and coordinated. We have described this relationship since the last decade as "co-makership"—a term used most often in Europe and as the English title of Giorgio Merli's (1993) book. The coordination of these relationships is called "supply chain management" which is discussed later in this chapter.

---

*When Americans talk about logistics, they mean the moving of goods from place to place. While when Europeans speak about logistics, they mean all materials' management, including scheduling, purchasing, shop-floor control, planning systems and physical movement.

This "pre-demand driven logistics" condition is also often called "supplier management." In the United States the term used is "Co-Op contracting." This term and its ideas grew out of the Just-in-Time movement.

On the surface the supplier management philosophy looks very much like others, for instance the Japanese *Kieretsu* idea, or the PECOs idea developed at General Motors in the early 1990s. But, it is not.

Simply stated, co-makership in the holonic business system is "A partnering philosophy and technique that complements the process-oriented approaches such as Just-in-Time manufacturing and Business Process Reengineering." All these approaches seek to define core business processes, eliminate wasteful activities and reduce lead times.

CO-MAKERSHIP: A SUPPLY STRATEGY FOR THE TWENTY-FIRST CENTURY

Manufacturing companies are finding increasingly that they must engage their suppliers as partners to achieve their strategic intent. Supplier equity is a "new" asset and in some businesses may be a core competence providing competitive advantage. Competitive advantage means the advantage a company has, due to one of five customer values: cost, quality, service, time or innovation.

Manufacturing businesses look at the world in one of two ways. "Product out," which focuses on the company's operations and products; or the new way "market in," which focuses on identifying the business opportunities posed by the marketplace and translating them into products the company could make, given its processes and capabilities. But even being a "market in" company is not enough if the business maintains an old-fashioned, rigid bureaucratic outlook.

Figure 5.1 shows a matrix of four manufacturing business organizing strategies.

Along with a "market in" orientation, it is also necessary to have a culture that is group oriented, rather than bureaucratic and hierarchical. Having the better of two alternatives in only one of the two dimensions does not do the job.

A company's outlook has a profound impact on how it operates in every way. The bureaucratic "product out" business—the

		Internal Organization	
		Bureaucratic Dynamics (Product Oriented)	Group Dynamics (Process Oriented)
Relationship with the Market	Operations Oriented	**A** Bureaucracy/ Product-out	**B** Involvement/ Process Improvement
	Market Oriented (Market-in)	**C** Marketing/ Product-in	**D** Venture Market-in

Figure 5.1 *Company organization strategy: the four alternatives*

Western company of the 1950s and the 1960s—believes it competes on its product and technology. Technologists find what the market needs, and the operationally oriented business makes it. While Western companies were shifting in the late 1970s and into the 1980s to more "market in" operations, they maintained a bureaucratic outlook. This meant that the locus of power and prestige merely shifted from the technologists to the marketeers. While, in the 1970s, the Japanese shifted their organization to a much more dynamic model. They maintained their internal focus, moving from a product orientation to a process orientation. Whether the Japanese left the issues of the marketplace behind is open to argument; clearly such companies as Sony, Panasonic, Toyota/Lexus and NEC have been quite attuned to the marketplace. But the main point is that Japanese management concentrated throughout all industries and all businesses on heightening their process capabilities.

Clearly, businesses that compete and win today and will continue to do so into the twenty-first century must be in the lower right box of the matrix (Figure 5.1). These businesses are both "market in" and dynamic oriented, in a venture/"market-in" position.

The logical extension of this "way of doing business" is to include both suppliers and customers within the value chain and the communication chain. You can see how the business is inevitably on a path toward creating a holonic network.

The relationship to suppliers within the "product out" way of working will be familiar to all who have worked in a manufacturing business. Many companies still operate this way today. They:

- exploit suppliers to the maximum;
- find subordinate and easily swayed suppliers;
- limit the information provided to suppliers;
- avoid binding or long-term agreements;
- purchase by single orders, each time setting up competition among suppliers.

It should be equally clear to anyone who has worked in a company trying to reshape itself as a "market in" company rather than a bureaucratic company that if the old fashioned supplier relationship model is followed, the effort is doomed to frustration and probably to failure.

At the beginning of 1994, Coopers & Lybrand conducted a study with the University of Michigan of automotive suppliers in the US. Suppliers were asked to rate OEMs—both the Big Three and Japanese transplants—on their degree of partnering with suppliers. A rating of five was the highest degree of partnering. The results were:

Toyota (US)	4.1
Chrysler	4.0
Nissan (US)	3.3
Ford	3.2
Honda (US)	3.0
General Motors	1.2

Clearly, some companies are not yet "walking the talk" when it comes to working closely with suppliers.

Venture/"market-in" businesses, take a medium- and long-term view of the market (a Japanese trait) and combine that with Western approaches of market analysis and a focus on innovation and product diversity. Their basis of competition is quality, lead time and flexibility, and they engage their partners up and down the value chain in discussions regarding those competitive aspects.

The supply strategies that venture/"market-in" businesses employ today put them on an inevitable path to the holonic business system. These strategies include:

- vertical integration of a logistic network to integrate suppliers and customers throughout the value chain;
- co-makership logic not just in operations, but in product design, in manufacturing key components and technologies, and in holistic business-generation;
- reduction of the supplier base to a few suppliers, tightly integrated into the business, which provides drastic cost reduction;
- creation of a common information system used for operations and deliveries and for planning, design and change management.
- outsourcing support and management processes to specialist companies.

In these businesses suppliers have moved from the conventional role beyond being an associated supplier—operational co-makership—to being a fully partnered supplier node as can be seen in Figure 5.2.

As a company moves from "partnering" to being a holon in a virtual company, its level of integration moves from one of being "involved" with the company it is supplying to one of being committed to the entire core business process—not just to the companies on either side.

But whether the relationship is one-on-one supplier to customer, or node-to-node within a holonic network where all nodes operate in the same way, the elements of this partnership are essentially the same.

Supplier Level	Quality	Logistics
Class III Conventional	• The supplier is responsible to furnish in accordance with quality specifications • The client makes incoming inspections and source inspections	• Supplies "order by phone" with specific delivery times • Reserve stocks necessary
Class II Associated	• Self-certification (supplier) • Free pass (client) • Quality improvement programs (supplier-client)	• Long-term contracts • JIT/synchronized deliveries directly to production departments (no stocks) • Continuous reduction of stocks and lead times (together)
Class I Partner	• The supplier is responsible for the conformity of components to the final customer satisfaction • Continuous improvement together • Co-design of quality requirements	• Supplier-integrated in the client's logistic process (same documents, same operative system) • Shared information and planning system (electronic data interchange network)
Class 0 Holonic Nodes	• Co-design virtual company business process	• Same information systems

Figure 5.2 *Supplier–customer operational model*

First, there is cooperation in designing new products and technologies. Suppliers are integrated into the customer's operations, and there is a feeling of mutual destiny—the supplier lives for the customer and the customer lives for the supplier's

Product and Technology Development	Node Choice Criteria
• Product and component characteristics designed solely by client • First supply verification	• Price
• Technical requirements of components and technology defined with supplier • Supplier consulted in advance	• Total cost
• Supplier involved in the development process, starting from product concept • Supplier involved in product planning process • Supplier proactive	• Speed
• Supplier commitment to product development and planning parocess	• Market innovation and support • Shared values • Flexibility

ability to live for his business. Increasingly, the customer's product components are based on the supplier's technology.

There is also a constant exchange of information concerning both products and processes. The client company's marketing people feed back information directly to the supplier company. This allows the partners to make quick, global decisions about any required product changes.

EUROPEAN CAR INDUSTRY: FORMAL AGREEMENTS THAT DEFINE WORKING ARRANGEMENTS

In Europe, the trade associations of the European automobile industry and the automotive supplier industry formalized their commitment to foster co-makership relationships. In April of 1994 the two associations forged the "European Guidelines for Cooperation between Automobile Manufacturers and their Suppliers," which focused on four specific areas:

1 Establishment of price/cost relationship
2 Cooperation in design and manufacturing planning
3 Effective adoption of modern manufacturing processes
4 Continuous quality improvement.

A full text of the agreement (see Table 5.1) shows that the relationship is one based on agreement and rules—it is too formal and lacks the trust expected in a true holonic network. This may be a deliberate "go-slow" approach. It could also be a cultural artifact for a continent in which incremental "by-the-book" steps are necessary to win buy-in from labor. European auto makers and their suppliers are not yet prepared for the inevitability of the holonic business system. The European Guidelines documented agreement is instructive in that it touches on the right issues, even if it does not answer them to the satisfaction of some.

US auto manufacturers are moving toward holonic business system in different ways, as you will see later in this chapter and in Chapter 8. The Japanese approach is to develop a "world car" with the major car companies contributing their best technology and everyone selling essentially the same product. One can envision that these three approaches—Japanese, US and European—will lead to a very different world of automotive production and competition by the first years of the twenty-first century.

Table 5.1 *European Guidelines for Cooperation between Automobile Manufacturers and their Suppliers*

PREAMBLE

In the face of globalization within the automotive industry and increasing worldwide competition, the European Automotive Industry must continue improvement in many key areas. The automotive manufacturers and their suppliers recognize the need to achieve adequate profitability to invest in new technologies and innovation to maintain World Class positions.

They recognize the mutual benefit derived from a close partnership between a manufacturer and a certain number of system suppliers. This equally requires a balanced structure, at the supplier level, between system suppliers and their subsystem suppliers.

This new partnership relationship between the automobile manufacturers and their suppliers is based upon an open dialogue and exchange of information throughout the supply chain. It enables all partners to strive towards continuous improvement or products and processes, in a spirit of mutual agreement.

These Guidelines do not aspire to establish a legal or contractual definition of the relationship between automobile manufacturers and their suppliers, but rather to determine the fundamental principles and set a recommended framework for cooperation within the European Automotive Industry.

The scope of the Guidelines covers the design and manufacture of automobiles, together with the supply of original equipment components. It is not the intention of this document to cover independent aftermarket issues, where the partners may operate separately.

1. **Cooperation in Design and Manufacturing Planning**
   - Automobile manufacturers and their suppliers should cooperate to establish an open, bilateral flow of relevant information on new products and processes, relating to the planning and decision-making processes during the concept and development phase. Both partners recognize and respect the sensitivity of this information.
   - The early involvement of suppliers in the development process should be encouraged.
   - The development service to be provided should be defined between the partners, by specifying the limits (definition of the areas of responsibility), and agreeing as to the payment for this service or supply.
   - The manufacturer should appoint the production supplier as early as possible in the development phase, so as to avoid duplication of effort and needless expense by both partners.
   - In appropriate areas, joint design or delegation of design responsibility to suppliers may take place, and where needed accompanied by guidance from the manufacturer.
   - Difficulties encountered in the manufacturer–supplier relationship (e.g. quality, cost, product, process, logistics, customer satisfaction) should be solved in a spirit of partnership. Either partner should feel free to identify problems. These problems should be discussed openly and tackled jointly for mutual benefit.

continued overleaf

Table 5.1   *(continued)*

- As soon as possible during the development phase, the partners should discuss warranty conditions as well as liability.

2. Price/Cost Relationship
- Both partners should promote a common method of price/cost analysis, taking into account the respective autonomy of each partner, and the transparency of relevant cost information. The total costs of products and processes should be understood throughout the supply chain and opportunities for improvement identified.
- Manufacturers and suppliers should endeavour to mutually agree target values, prices and conditions for parts or services as early as possible during the concept phase.
- Partners should mutually agree on the appropriate price modifications stemming from changes in specifications or additional requirements (e.g. logistics, warranty) insofar as they have an influence on the costs.
- Both partners should aim at continuous quality improvement and cost reduction during both the development phase and the actual production of the part. The partners may consider that design changes could be appropriate to achieve this result, and if so will cooperate fully to this effect.
- The benefits of successful cost reduction should be enjoyed by both partners, based on a balanced understanding of the source of the cost decrease.

3. Effective Adoption of Modern Manufacturing Processes
- Recognizing the potential improvements to competitiveness stemming from the adoption of simultaneous engineering processes, both partners should strive to increase and improve the application of such processes.
- As appropriate, vehicle manufacturers may initiate technical assistance programmes to help suppliers adopt new manufacturing methods and improve productivity and quality. Where needed, such technical assistance programmes may include cooperative training.

4. Quality
- Automobile manufacturers and their suppliers should strive to adopt a common European approach to quality within a jointly defined framework.
- A joint commitment to total quality improvement on all fronts and at all levels should be made by both partners.
- Duplication of quality assessment work should be avoided through intercompany cooperation.

5. Logistics
- Automobile manufacturers and their suppliers should endeavour to develop and incorporate Electronic Data Interchange concepts and attempt to produce a common European system.

Table 5.1 *(continued)*

- Throughout the supply chain, all functions should aim at minimizing unexpected schedule fluctuations, recognizing the need to manage changes required to meet market demands.
- Any changes should be swiftly communicated to the suppliers, using EDI wherever practical.

6. Legal Rules
- If agreed at the outset, multi-annual contracts should contain a "renegotiation" clause, which would apply in the event of extraordinary and unforeseen cost changes.
- Changes in prices and conditions should only apply to previously negotiated contracts, with the agreement of both parties.
- Project-related information should be treated as sensitive and confidential. Design information (including CAD data, product/process know-how, process FMEA (failure, mode and effect analysis) should not be disclosed without mutual consent. Exceptions must be contracted for, in detail, and take into account the interests of both partners.
- Automobile manufacturers and their suppliers should respect each other's intellectual property rights.
- The partners shall search for a mutually acceptable agreement regarding the use of their Brand Marks.

Done in Brussels, April 12, 1994

For the auto makers, G. Garuzzo
For the suppliers, E. K. Planchon

That world may be one in which global holonic networks consist of the same suppliers geographically positioned near the assemblers. Or it may consist of regional networks, where each node uses common tooling. Either way, the arrival of the world car would make the holonic business system more inevitable. The major question then becomes how to get a true world car in a prosumer-dominated market.

CHOOSING A CO-MAKERSHIP PARTNER (THE CO-OP METHODOLOGY)

Choosing suppliers to be co-makership partners—or members of a holonic network—involves both evaluating their ability to meet current requirements for quality and lead time and their "willingness" to continually improve.

In co-makership, many companies use a supplier certification program to create a universe of suppliers. Quality is set at a level of bad parts per million (PPM). Lead time is set with a goal for a continuous reduction in lead time. Such a goal might be to reduce 50 percent per year until total lead time, minus shipping time, is equal to twice the value added time in production.

The customer must map its internal processes and understand them, for if you do not understand your processes fully you cannot understand how a potential supplier's processes will fit with yours in the "shared destiny" of co-makership or a holonic network.

The most critical activity in the undertaking of a partnership agreement is the supplier visit. The purpose of this visit is not to evaluate a supplier, but to understand the supplier's process of manufacture and the associated support and management processes. A visit should identify the opportunities for generic lead time reduction, quality issues, cost development and raw material continuum. The data gathered from such visits will be the basis for development of the real lead times, process costs and profit distribution for the node.

A supplier visit is an exercise in "routing by walking around." You need to walk the route of the core business process, talking to the individuals who carry out the activities. The team making the visit should follow the actual flows from the point when the order or release first arrives in the mail room. Orders may arrive by phone or a demand signal from the arrival of an upstream component. Do not take someone's word for how the process is supposed to work—follow the route exactly. If you are dealing with a group of products made by the supplier that have been grouped into a "commodity," then follow the route of each sub-commodity separately. Calculate all queues to get a true idea of real lead times, not published or purported times. You need to get specific data regarding the following:

- Process knowledge, including flows, changeover times, changeover frequencies, lot-sizing rules and problems.
- Quality and yields, especially yield variances from lot to lot.
- Raw material's continuum.
- Paperwork flow.

- Competition for capacity that could potentially be dedicated to the network.
- Pricing structures in sufficient detail to develop process costs.

By the end of the visit you should have estimated opportunities concerning lead time, quality, traffic and logistics and cost and tooling and packaging.

By understanding both your own processes and the processes of your potential partners, you can answer the question, "How can I as the downstream customer make things easier for the supplier?" Remember, you and the supplier are entering a "shared destiny," where the supplier will live for you and you will live for the supplier's ability to live for you.

Within a holonic network, the relationship may not be a team from the customer visiting one supplier. It will be the network initiator and a team from some companies acting as nodes or thinking of becoming nodes in the network who will visit a company that would like to become a node, or visiting each other's nodes to understand better the processes and how they all tie together to give a "synergy of value".

APPLYING CO-MAKERSHIP IN AN AUTOMOTIVE SUPPLIER

This example concerns a business which is a major UK-based manufacturer of safety-critical hydraulic assemblies for the automotive industry. It has in-house operations encompassing precision machining, electroplating, system assembly and testing. The company designs, develops and supplies complete vehicle systems for a range of vehicle OEMs' customers. It also supplies replacement parts.

The company is not a global player, although as an old-established operation it has a well-known brand of considerable value. It has three competitors besides certain vehicle OEMs who continue to make their components in-house. Each competitor has significantly greater volume, and an increasingly technically-superior product. They have forced the business to move away from volume, and into niche markets where their specific product technology is more suited. The business has also responded at the strategic level by exploiting the profitable but short-lived opportunity represented by a large domestic UK vehicle park. These vehicles carry their parts as original fit.

The business has been under serious cost pressure for over a decade. Losing money fast in the early 1980s, it returned to profit through slashing headcount and exploiting the high margins generated in the aftermarket business. It also subcontracted most of its turning operations, a major change as the business had one of the largest turned parts production facilities in Europe.

On the appointment of a new Operations Director late in 1992, manufacturing, purchasing and supply were put under the spotlight. A new purchasing manager also joined the company around the same time.

Purchased parts, at around $60 million per annum, is the single largest portion of operating cost. It is split into 25 percent raw materials for machining, principally castings and bars and 75 percent other components, including plastic and rubber moldings, pressings, fasteners and precision machined parts.

The focus of relationships with suppliers for decades had been to seek lowest prices. Meanwhile, the suppliers had seen volumes fall, and the maintenance of fixed tooling (for presswork, for example) stopped in the drive to save money. For many suppliers, supplying the business was no longer profitable. The business was difficult to deal with. Its people were tough negotiators and deaf to ideas. Furthermore the business was poor at scheduling, and the perpetrator of many disjointed initiatives over the years.

These weaknesses affected the suppliers too. It was found that 62 percent of the supplier base of 400 companies was ranked for financial security as "above normal risk." Furthermore fewer than one in five suppliers were ISO9000 accredited.

The Purchasing Department was the elephant's graveyard— the place where non-achievers were sent. The atmosphere was one of a resigned acceptance of their fate, and not one where a talented individual would thrive. The jobs of buying, and expediting supply, were combined. An assessment of staff age, length of service and salary against awareness of supply issues revealed alarming gaps and misalignment.

Over the next two years, the new management team carried out a revolution. This came from a "clean sheet of paper" review of the way the business might manage suppliers and achieve improvements.

The main elements that the team identified were the following needs:

- To define and install a new set of supplier selection and retention criteria—moving away from being price-driven and toward being cost-driven.
- To use the selection and retention criteria as the basis for every sourcing decision.
- To move away from a purchasing office organized around commodities, to a team focused on relationships.
- To reduce the number of active supplier accounts.
- To reduce radically the internal costs of dealing with suppliers, including all handling, inspection and engineering support required to get a usable component at the point of use.
- To reduce materials prices yet again, by at least 3 percent per year, just to keep up with the sales price reductions that were being given to OEMs.

Changes began and, first, the supplier selection criteria were set up. The buyers were educated in what this meant, both for analysis and as a tool for reshaping the supplier base. Senior managers in finance, engineering, marketing and manufacturing were also educated. The message was simple, "we are moving away from price-driven, to focus on internal cost, and you should understand what this means for you!" Suppliers were measured formally against the new criteria and then ranked by their achievements against them. This identified some early opportunities.

Next, the Purchasing Department was restructured resembling "procurement positioning." This meant separating buyers and suppliers according to nature of the relationship. At the extremes, this split those suppliers who were very important from those supplying items where there was great latitude in being able to hunt for sundry commodities. Critical suppliers are locked in by design and a partnership is mandatory. In the middle, there were segments recognizing shades of grey about the ability of either party to move away from the relationship. In these there is balance of power concerning their mutual importance as trading partners.

Once restructured, the buyers developed clear objectives for their segment, and expressed them in a supplier development plan. Each buyer was now measured on how well his suppliers met the selection criteria.

The third initiative was the clustering of suppliers in certain categories, and the creation of the main supplier idea. A good example concerned turned parts, which were sourced to 10 suppliers. One of them, who met the selection criteria best was approached and asked if he would run the whole turned parts enterprise for the business. He did not have to manufacture all the turned parts but could leave the other existing arrangements intact if he wanted. However, he would have to take full responsibility for supply and pricing. This gave the business a large reduction in the number of suppliers that it dealt with. It also gave the main supplier latitude to configure the supply, and gave him a volume benefit. Some reshuffling of supply did occur and the second tier of suppliers was cut to seven. The main supplier took over bar purchasing for the holonic network, and got a price reduction which was shared with the business.

The main supplier concept was rolled out to packaging, fastenings and small consumable tools within a year. The fastenings' main supplier also was the model for a completely new logistic approach. It took on full responsibility for 28 sub-suppliers, and did not manufacture at all itself. This approach provided a radical and first-class logistic service. It coordinated supply into the depot, to stock levels which the fastenings' main supplier figured out. It also delivered twice daily direct to the point of use in the business's plant. The supplier used kanbans to signal the need to replenish. Service level availability shot up, and the supplier was paid a premium over the original price of the component. The business took out all of the internal cost and complexity associated with fasteners that were considered as sundry, trivial unit value, items.

The business also devolved responsibility for quality, and moved from a rigorous component-by-component quality evaluation. It was replaced by a system that assured the supplier's business process, and after that trusted the supplier. The system evaluation was underpinned by the selection criteria, of course. The tedious paperwork associated with validations, revalidation and retests was eliminated. This left the supplier only to confirm that the components met the design criteria.

The last piece of the jigsaw was the one that really changed the way of working with suppliers. It brought all the actions described above into a coherent whole. It mirrored the co-makership approach. It was the development of a closed-loop cost-reduction process, applied only to those suppliers identified as security-critical for procurement. The logic was that both parties would plot a cost–time graph, exposing how the cost of the item built up. This was done first in the supplier's process and then in the business as it made or built the product. The two sides agreed what each was doing that influenced and drove up the costs in the other's process. Having done that they would agree actions, and precisely what saving this would bring in unit cost and throughput time. They then went away, to carry out an agreed schedule of changes, supporting each other if necessary. Once the cycle was complete, price could be addressed in a positive context, and the benefits shared.

The psychology was perfect. Instead of price being at the top of the agenda, it was subordinated and replaced by discussions of cost, mutual help and successes. To make the process work, the buyers had to be retrained, in how to assess and understand processes and business economics, and how to manage projects.

Overall, the results were spectacular. For the first time, component prices fell by 5 percent. This was strange, considering that the whole idea had been not to focus on price. Internal costs were halved. The buyers were changed people. One man, who was marked down as a complete no-hoper, improved greatly. His supplier base was identified as responsible for 60 percent of the $1.5 million of cost reductions achieved in the first year. The second year identified over another $1.5 million of benefits that could be put down to co-makership actions.

PROCESS COSTING

Holonic networks make extensive use of a technique called process costing as it understands the way the core business processes of each node are combined into virtual companies.

Process costing is based on activity-based costing (ABC). ABC is used primarily to figure out better the real cost of existing products, instead of merely "peanut buttering" overhead costs on top of direct labor hours across the array of products. ABC reapportions the overhead costs to the array of products in a way that more accurately reflects the relationship between overhead activities as they relate to specific products.

Process costing estimates the cost of the core business processes required to produce and deliver a product. It has two major applications within a holonic network.

First, process costing provides the virtual company with a clear definition of the business process cost drivers and their relationship to the design details. This allows the integrator to understand how these cost drivers affect design decisions. Second, it serves as input into the formulae that will be used for establishing the final product price, and just as important, the profit allocation for each node.

The first step in developing a process cost is to strip away the non-value-adding activities within the core business process. These would be identified during the initial visits by the network initiator to each node in the holonic network—or each node wishing to join in a virtual company that is being established.

Such non-value-adding activities may include, for example, sales and marketing, design of in-house products, materials planning and procurement. The costs of the remaining activities are then broken down and assigned to specific activities in much the same way as in an ABC analysis. The difference is that, in process costing, the costs are assigned only to a core business process.

Finally, specific costs of the holonic network, such as travel, tooling, virtual product design time, management time to support the network, and so on, are added back as an overhead distributed as a fixed percentage. The result of the calculation is a rate per hour for the holon's usage.

Now let us see how demand-driven logistics acts to strip away non-value-adding activities throughout the virtual company and creates the proper atmosphere for products to move through the virtual company with alacrity.

TWO TYPES OF DEMAND-DRIVEN LOGISTICS

Demand-driven logistics is the tangible glue that binds the holonic network together. There are two types of demand-driven logistics. One is sequential, as in an OEM automotive assembler, who sends signals back through the supply chain to component manufacturers and subassemblers who produce in sequence of final assembly. The other is the demand replacements for goods, as in the retail industry.

In both cases there is an electronic signal that reserves capacity. That can be one set of car seats for the automotive OEM and one bottle of soda for the grocery retailer. The party that controls the demand point says, in effect, "I'll tell you exactly what I need when I need it (e.g. a red seat or a blue seat; a bottle of cola or a bottle of root beer or a bottle of orange soda) but for now just hold the capacity."

CONVENTIONAL LOGISTICS

Conventional logistics is characterized by a series of discontinuous steps or locations within the material continuum. Since the 1950s, information systems have been put in place and continually honed to manage this discontinuity. Today, however, innovative leaders in supply-line techniques challenge the assumption that such discontinuity needs to exist.

Distribution requirements planning (DRP), master production scheduling (MPS), materials requirements planning (MRP), and a host of other technological attempts to smooth logistics have all been tried. But if the discontinuity can be abolished, all that would be needed is reserved capacity and the final assembly schedule (FAS), which tells the node what to make in the shortest possible—or real—value added lead time.

Even in the best companies that employ MRP systems, the elapsed time is two or more weeks from distribution center shipment to shop or purchase order generation, because most MRP systems are regenerated in weekly or monthly periods.

The technology and scheduling time needed reinforces the need for warehouses and buffer stocks. The existence of such inventory beyond the demand times requires forecasting, which

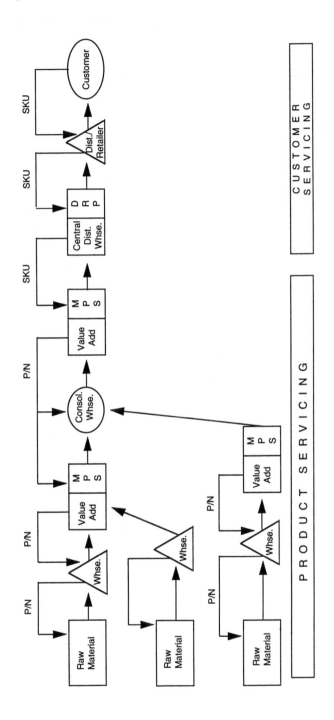

Figure 5.3 *Conventional logistics path*

in turn virtually assures that the factory will be making something for which there is no immediate demand. As each more sophisticated MRP system is installed, the amount of discontinuity is heightened. This leads to companies being trapped in the "X"RP mentality, constantly seeking the next, more sophisticated planning tool.

Compounding this "slow response" scenario, the traffic department recommends full transport loads (FTLs), which represent days or weeks of consumption. Figure 5.3 shows a conventional logistics path, from raw materials to the final customer.

Just-in-Time manufacturing within a company's four walls can only go so far to increasing responsiveness. This has been shown time and again in Western companies that have undertaken JIT since it became popular in the 1980s. The few companies that have successfully broken the lead time inflation cycle through the materials continuum have done so by working closely with both suppliers and customers. They have tightened the value chain both up and down stream.

A 1988 review of the materials continuum for the catalytic converter at a US auto assembler showed four main operations in the production cycle: ceramic honeycomb block, noble metal coating, canning—encasing the coated block in a metal jacket— and OEM assembly. The inventory throughout the value chain was the equivalent of 250 days. Analysis showed that if demand-driven logistics were set up, coupled with other improvements such as product rationalization and quality improvements, cost to the OEM would be reduced by 31 percent and inventory throughout the supply chain would be reduced to seven days.

SUPPLY CHAIN MANAGEMENT

The key to demand-driven logistics is not technological, it has to do with management behavior. Many companies are attempting to get control over lead times through what is known as supply chain management, which sets predefined performance parameters. Supply chain management, which is becoming a more common practice, especially in retail companies, has 10 characteristics. Some characteristics are the same as those in demand-driven logistics, yet some are different:

1   *Predefined players.* This is the idea of setting up long-term arrangements, rather than putting each new purchase out to competitive bid. This is key to both supply chain management and demand-driven logistics.

2   *Predefined working rules with respect to inventory, lead times and delivery frequency.* Demand-driven logistics sets rules about who will hold inventory, and has predefined lead times, but keys delivery to signals sent back to fulfil, rather than defining up-front when goods will be delivered.

3   *Each player takes care of its own inventory.* This is the same in demand-driven logistics.

4   *Sequential and fixed activities.* In demand-driven logistics within a holonic network there must be flexibility for the purchaser to go to one or more nodes.

5   *Known product catalogues.* In demand-driven logistics suppliers reserve capacity, and are told what to produce at the last possible moment. Rather than a catalogue of parts, there is the ability to make what is required.

6   *Continually balancing cost and service.* In demand-driven logistics associated with holonic networks there is no trade-off. Service is everything, and it is up to the node and the integrator to control cost, since the market sets the price.

7   *Strategically oriented—set up to achieve strategic goals.* Demand-driven logistics is tactical, in that it is an enabler of the strategic imperatives of speed and reduced exposure to inventory costs and product obsolescence.

8   *Leadership occurs at downstream operations.* In a holonic network, leadership resides with the integrator, wherever the integrator resides. However, demand is managed at the downstream location by demand-driven logistics and real consumption.

9   *Consumption data is given to all participants.* This is an absolute must in a demand-driven logistics environment. But in demand-driven logistics this sharing of data goes even further, to a sharing of market strategies among the nodes throughout the holonic network.

10 *Handles a physical product.* Demand-driven logistics does not need a physical product. For example, in a bank supporting a car dealership, the customer pulls the approval process.

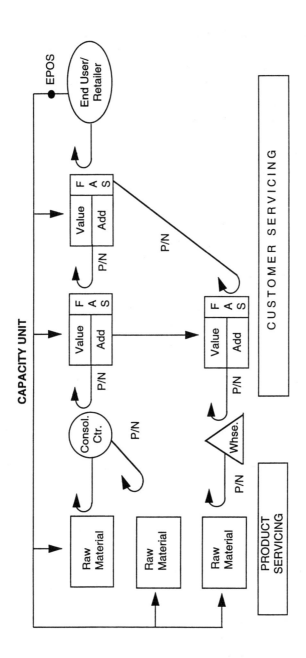

Figure 5.4 *Demand-driven logistics.*

KEYING LOGISTICS TO CAPACITY

The key to demand-driven logistics is the concept of capacity. A diagrammatic representation of demand-driven logistics is shown is Figure 5.4.

The basic tenets of demand-driven logistics are:

1 Buy capacity, not SKUs;
2 Capacity units should be synchronously pulled through the supply chain.
3 Capacity must be flexible to meet real demand.
4 Final assembly schedule FAS replaces traditional MPS and MRP.
5 Minimum lead times throughout the value chain. Value add time, queue time and transport time have to be reduced. This argues for geographic proximity usually, or at least for close partnering with "the best" mover of goods.
6 A bill of resources is tied to the traditional bill of material and both are exploded simultaneously through the asset manager. This is discussed later in this chapter.

THE THEORY BEHIND DEMAND-DRIVEN LOGISTICS

Companies have warehouses because they make product in large lot sizes to a forecast. The basic techniques of Just-in-Time manufacturing—setup reduction, flexible tooling and simple machines in work cells—allow for manufacturing in smaller lot sizes.

If a company continues to forecast and make specific SKUs to that forecast, it is certain that items will be made for which there is no immediate demand. This is because forecasts, by definition, are always wrong at the SKU level.

Forecasts are more accurate overall than they are at the SKU level. And the shorter the period to real demand the more accurate the forecast. For example, a forecast for men's shorts two months before Fathers' Day in the US is far more accurate than a forecast for 36 inch waist blue denim shorts seven months out.

Most manufacturers see lumpy demand at the SKU *level*, so they protect themselves by establishing a backlog and maintaining inventory. In reality, most aggregate demand is relatively stable—orders of magnitude more stable than at the SKU level.

For example, most manufacturing companies establish a production schedule that says that the company will produce so many units of output per day, for a period—usually one month or a quarter. These production plans reflect aggregate demand. Where the plan goes awry is at the specific SKU level. Customers just do not order what is made at the time it is made.

At the aggregate level, the production plan has, in effect, stated a capacity requirement for the future. If you are a supplier to that production plan you know that for every unit of output by the customer you will supply "x" units of input.

You do not need to know what the specific unit is that you will supply three months ahead of when it must be delivered to the customer; you just need to know that you have agreed by accepting the aggregate production plan to have so much capacity available every day so that you can make what is required by your customer's real demand. In this way, the customer and the supplier have agreed to "buy" or "sell" capacity, rather than specific SKU.

Once the backlog queues have been turned into reserved capacity at each stage in the value chain, then the time that it really takes to add value to a product is the real lead time. In practice, this is usually only 5 percent of the current actual lead time.

Suppose, for example, that you supply disk drives to MEGA-PC the fictional company we described in Chapter 1. The real time to assemble and test a drive is about 10 minutes. Component manufacture is about 30 minutes and transport time is 240 minutes. Therefore, 280 minutes before MEGA-PC is going to assemble a custom-ordered PC (one eight-hour shift, or the previous day) an EDI message is sent to the drive manufacturer that specifies which drive has been ordered by the customer.

Up until that point, the drive supplier only knew that MEGA-PCs production plan was to make 3000 units per day, at that rate the average PC has 1.1 drives/units. Therefore, the drive supplier has reserved the capacity to manufacture 3300 drives each day for MEGA-PC.

Unfortunately, customers do not conform to even the best production plans, so MEGA-PC asks suppliers to hold a "window" of +/– 15 percent on a daily basis. This means that on any given day it could ask you to manufacture from 2850 to 3750 drives. In order for suppliers to be able to arrange that flexibility, they must track actual shipments from MEGA-PC. Therefore, the need for the capacity reservation signal sent to all suppliers throughout the value chain.

Some industries have more radical demand spikes than +/– 15 percent. Soft drinks, for instance, experience wide demand swings, especially to the upside in hot weather. In our previous book (Johansson *et al.*, 1993) we told how Coca-Cola and Schweppes Beverages Limited in the UK built a more flexible factory, and kept spare capacity to adapt to these spikes. The key is that the extra capacity was designed into the value chain. Inventory, on the other hand, is not flexible and costs more to carry on an ongoing basis than the extra capacity built into the value chain.

In demand-driven logistics, rather than operating through a set of rules developed by the supply chain management group, the market sets the rules, and they are constantly changing. There is no tradeoff between cost and service; in a demand-driven logistics world costs are minimized while service is maximized.

Demand-driven logistics is further driven by the philosophy that minimum lead times should be maintained throughout the materials' chain; that transportation and warehousing add no value, only cost; and that all upstream demand signals should emanate simultaneously from the point of sale via electronic data interchange.

DEMAND REPLACEMENT IN PRACTICE

In mid-1992 the Grocery Manufacturers of America, Inc., a trade association, initiated an industry-wide effort it called Efficient Consumer Response (ECR). This is an industry strategy that seeks to create a seamless supply chain of retailers, distributors and suppliers. Through this supply chain it provides grocery customers with better products, assortments, in-stock service, convenience and price.

ECR takes as its starting point Quick Response (QR), the approach taken by such retailers as Wal-Mart in the US, and Sainsbury and Tesco in the UK. QR replenishes one SKU when it is consumed. In the US, such a system had also been set up between suppliers and the so-called warehouse "club" retailers—Price Club, Sam's, Costco, BJ's, and others.

Traditional retailers complained that suppliers were giving the clubs preferential pricing. The suppliers said it was easier doing business with the clubs and less costly because of the replenishment policies and practices established. They appreciated the essentially stable ordering and demand-driven logistics. After studying the issue, the grocery association was forced to adopt it, putting its own spin on it and calling it ECR.

Although QR goes only one level deep—the signal to replenish an SKU goes from the retailer to the first tier supplier—for an industry to adopt such a practice so quickly is radical.

ECR seeks to take this principle to the entire supply chain in true demand-driven logistics fashion. EDI transfer from the point of sale (e.g. the cash register ringing up a two-liter bottle of a particular type of soft drink made by a particular company) sends signals to the company's filling line, the bottlemaking company, the cap making company and the label making company.

Besides efficient replenishment, ECR seeks to have efficient store assortment, efficient promotion and efficient product introduction. Modern information systems make this possible.

With point-of-sale data fed back through the system, distributors no longer need to "sell into" the system using special pricing and coupons all of which erode margins. Rather consumption becomes the driver for replenishment. Suppliers, manufacturers and distributors with accurate store-level movement and demographic data help bring this about, as does proper space management and category management.

Reengineering promotions is being undertaken to cut promotion costs, and to even off what has been in the past promotion-driven variability in much of the retail–supplier relationship. Wal-Mart pioneered this effort with its "always lowest price," idea, trading away trade promotions with its suppliers in exchange for a consistent low price, while the supplier enjoys smooth demand, and thus more efficient manufacturing and distribution activities.

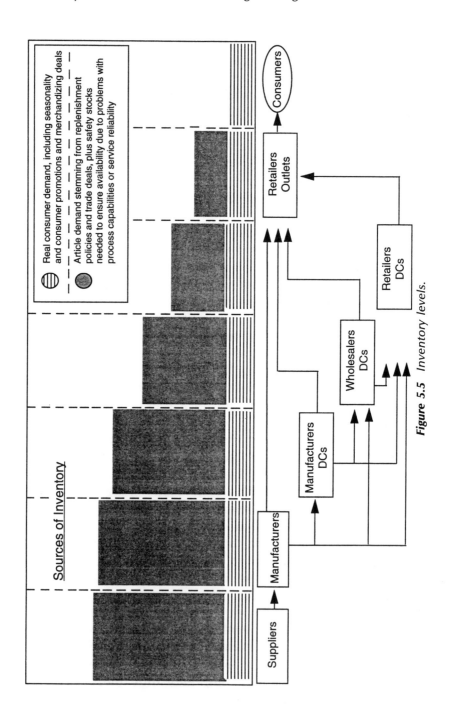

Figure 5.5 *Inventory levels.*

By sharing the risks of new product introductions among all supply chain players, it is hoped that the ECR strategy will lead to fewer product extensions and "me-too" products, and to more true innovations.

Figure 5.5 shows inventory through the typical consumer good demand fulfilment pipeline. ECR strategies seek to eliminate the distortions represented by the dark shaded area.

OEM SEQUENTIAL DEMAND-DRIVEN LOGISTICS

Beginning in 1989, one US auto maker sought to create a demand-driven logistics environment in its repair parts replenishment process. As part of the company's quality improvement effort, it found the growing frustration of customers who had to go back a second time for a repair because a part was not available the first time. Studies have long shown that "repair frustration" is a leading cause of American consumers switching car manufacturers.

The company's "stock outs" at the nearest distribution point was 7 percent, about the industry average, but deemed unacceptable by company executives, especially given that the company had $5 billion in spares inventory—almost one full year of dollar demand.

There were two main reasons for the high inventory. First, if the spare was a current production part, the manufacturers who made the part were loathe to interrupt regular production flow to service "lumpy" spares' demand. Second, if the part was not for current production models, the tooling was usually sent to an after market supplier, who set large lot sizes for economies of manufacture with unfamiliar tooling that was not created for flexible runs.

Our analysis for this company showed the average lead time to be 180 days—with the longest lead time coming from Japanese partner suppliers. That was for simple replenishment. On top of that, the company held safety stock of two-thirds the lot size, meaning another 120 days of inventory, or a total lead time of 300 days.

The company set as its goal to reengineer the spares replenishment process to increase the "customer fill rate" to

98 percent (reduce the stock outs from 7 to 2 percent) and reduce the inventory by 20 percent, or $1 billion.

The company was able to exceed both goals, following a few simple demand-driven logistics principles:

1   Get the stock quantity as close to the ultimate demand as possible, to smooth out perceived demand variance. The closer to the real demand the more stable the demand becomes. It is the large lot sizes and long lead times that make demand appear unpredictable.
2   Buy smoothed capacity at the suppliers, reduce their real lead time, and firm up the specific SKU at the shortest possible lead time.
3   Design the parts to commit to final specification at the latest possible time.
4   Where possible, reduce the number of stocking points so that the aggregate forecast is more accurate.

While some of these principles appear antithetical to each other, when one analyzes the entire value chain the principles can be judiciously applied.

First, the company mapped the typical supply chain for repair and replacement parts, which is shown in Figure 5.6.

In this old way of doing business, each part came from the manufacturer—either an auto company factory or an outside supplier factory—into the company's central distribution warehouse. From there, it either went to one of the company's 18 regional warehouses or to the central distribution warehouse of a third party parts seller such as ADAP. Outside manufacturers also sell their products directly to the parts sellers.

From the third party seller's central distribution warehouse, it would go to a retail outlet then to the end user, a home repair customer or an independent service station. Some local dealerships also buy from parts service stores.

From a company's regional warehouses, the particular part would travel to master dealers around the country. A master dealer is a large dealership from which smaller local dealerships can obtain parts. In this way, any dealership can obtain any part in inventory at a master dealer either the same day or in one day, rather than having a customer wait maybe

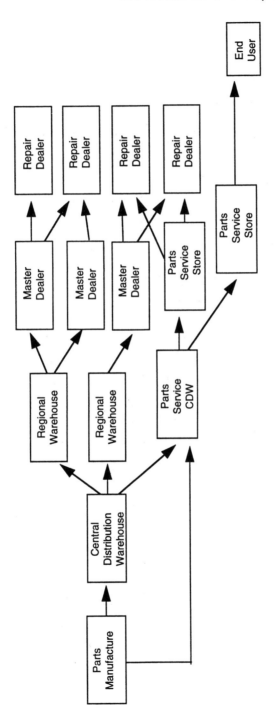

Figure 5.6 *Typical supply chain for repair and replacement parts*

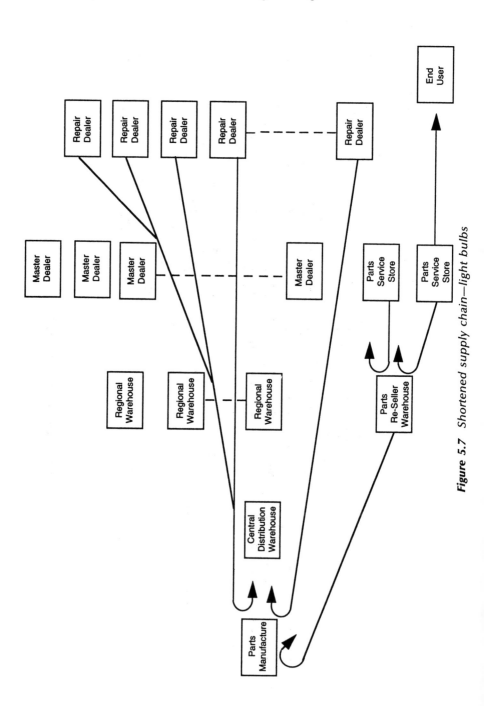

Figure 5.7 *Shortened supply chain—light bulbs*

a few days for a part to arrive from a regional warehouse. There are thousands of local repair dealers in this company's network, as well as thousands of independent repair shops.

As the company studied ways to compress the supply chain, it realized first that the supply chain needed to become more flexible to fit different types of parts. Some parts could and should move in one way from the manufacturer to the customer's car and others would need a different route.

Figure 5.7 shows the shortened supply chain for commodity-type items like light bulbs, which are inexpensive and have a large demand.

In this instance, a small quantity of items can be stocked at each local repair dealership. While the dealership orders the part from the OEM, the demand-driven logistics signal goes directly to the light bulb manufacturer. Parts' manufacturers ship directly to the repair dealerships.

The auto company serves as an integrator for this transaction, providing support and service at the point of interface between the manufacturer and each individual dealer. The company also bills the local dealer. Trust between the OEM and the parts' manufacturer prevents the latter from billing the local dealer directly at a higher margin.

Figure 5.8 shows the company's vision for a higher priced item with less frequent demand, namely a red fender for a company model. But for the car maker and its dealer network, the manufacturer merely makes fenders, which are held in stock at the company's central distribution warehouse. When the order comes from a local repair dealer for a red fender (or a blue one, or a yellow one, etc.) the fender is painted at the central distribution warehouse and shipped directly to the repair dealer.

Knowing that its core competence within the business of providing repair and replacement parts is not painting body parts, the car maker has brought in another company—Pittsburgh Paint and Glass. This company ran the paint booth at the central distribution warehouse and in effect become a holon node physically located inside another node.

This scheme allows the company to provide three–five day service for replacement body parts to its dealers' body shops, which is usually acceptable for bodywork customers. Some body shops order the unpainted fender and paint it themselves.

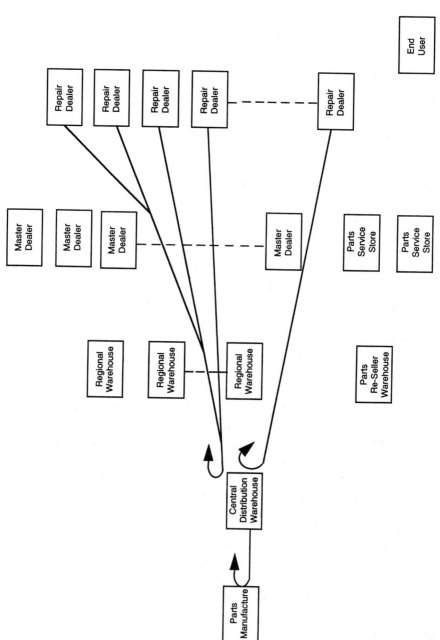

Figure 5.8 Supply chain for item with infrequent demand—red fender

While three days is acceptable to wait for a new fender to repair a damaged car, customers expect an oil pump to be replaced the day the car is brought in. Figure 5.9 shows the way the company envisions a tightened supply chain that reaches this goal.

Here, the parts manufacturers ship directly to master dealers. Oil pumps are too large, and too costly, for each local repair dealer to keep in stock, but they must be available on a same day basis. Also, the car maker knows sales of various car models by region, and knows from engineering data the mean-time-between-failures of oil pumps, but it does not know which local dealer any particular customer will drive to (or more likely be towed to) in case of an oil pump failure.

In its role as integrator, the car maker maintains specifications and warrantee paperwork.

The company's vision of the supply chain for a recall item is similar to a commodity item such as light bulbs, except that the manufacturer of the part will push the item to the local dealers, rather than stocking and waiting for their pull signals.

In defining the scope of supply chain compression, the company asked itself a simple question: "What is the customer's expectation of having this repair or replacement accomplished?"

For a light bulb, the customer expects to have it done in five minutes; if the bulb is not available the customer will go somewhere else to have it put in—and maybe go to another place the next time work is needed.

For an oil pump, the customer expects to have the repair completed the day the car is brought into the dealership or service station.

For the red fender, the customer can often wait a few days and bring the car in "by appointment." Or, if the car is not drivable, customers expect complete body work to take a few days.

After defining the customer expectation, and coupling it with the objectives of better service and lower inventories, the company set about rationalizing the number of suppliers so that it could negotiate stable capacity buys. In one example, the after-market company that stamps fenders, hoods, etc., reduced its lead time from 18 weeks to five days. It did this by providing a dedicated line to the OEM, in exchange for the stability of capacity buying. The stamping company, in effect, created a separate line to become a holonic node within the virtual company

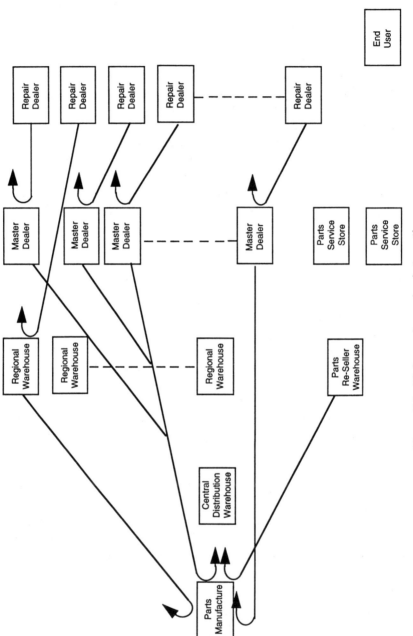

Figure 5.9 *Tightened supply chain—oil pump*

set up to produce spare body parts for the OEM. In its first two years of carrying out compressed supply chains for most items, the auto company took $1 billion out of what had been $5 billion in inventory. Also it improved the customer order fill rate to 99 percent—and customer satisfaction ratings greatly. More spectacularly, the company closed eight of the eighteen regional distribution centers, thus consolidating the forecast error toward a more stable demand profile.

ASSET MANAGEMENT

Managing the daily production schedule of fenders coming into the central distribution warehouse from a supplier—or even a handful of suppliers—should not be an onerous task for the car company.

But what about managing the daily production schedules of dozens—or even hundreds—of companies producing a myriad of light bulbs and shipping them to local dealers around the country and perhaps around the world?

Or what about scheduling the production of 50 000 pieces— half of them custom pieces—that go into one customer-designed house manufactured by the Sikisui company and its holonic network? What about scheduling those 50 000 pieces times 10 houses, or 100 houses, which are designed each day at one of the company's design centers?

To do this, a company needs to create an asset manager information system, often using artificial intelligence. The asset manager provides the mechanism for accepting and scheduling every order every day for manufacture the same day or the next day. By reducing planning and lead times to a minimum, the point of manufacture for any particular part becomes inconsequential. By first "pulling capacity" and then specific SKU, the company can issue daily production orders and be assured of minimum lead time delivery.

The asset manager requires a set of key data bases, including manufacturing and design specifications, and quality requirements and procedures. The asset manager is also used to provide data to the accounting and control functions.

In holonic networks that provide products with many suppliers for components and subassemblies, the rules by which the asset manager will work need to be addressed in the network design. These rules include how the asset manager will choose a supplier—by random, by region, by filling one supplier's capacity first them moving on to the next?

ADDING VALUE IN TRANSPORT

Although the demand-driven logistics philosophy argues that transportation adds no value, some businesses have been able to find ways to add value during transportation by locating value added operations on the transport vehicles.

Cement mixers, for instance, have long incorporated the process of mixing cement and the act of driving the cement to the construction sites. Besides, it is tough to pour hardened cement!

Fruits and vegetables are often picked unripened for long shipments; some companies have added ultraviolet lights to their transport vehicles to provide a more natural ripening environment, rather than having the produce arrive hard and ripen on the shelf. In this way excess inventory is avoided.

Electronics assemblies require "burn in" that can take from hours to days. Why does this burn in have to occur on a shelf at the factory? Why not on a truck taking the assemblies to the final destination? The quarantine period against bacterial contamination in pharmaceuticals can be accomplished during transport from the manufacturing site in Puerto Rico to the port of US mainland entry in Baltimore.

Perhaps the most innovative attempt to add value to transportation has been made by Frito-Lay. To provide the freshest product to grocery shelves, and more importantly because the product is so light and bulky—like transporting bags of air that is more costly to transport than it is to produce—the company produces locally. Route drivers pick up product every day for delivery. Here demand-driven logistics does not require electronic transfer of data. The route driver merely replenishes the bags taken the day before.

It should be clear from this discussion that co-makership and demand-driven logistics are, in many ways, the glue that holds together a holonic network that is engaged in production, transportation and sales of physical products.

6
More Systems within the System—Outsourcing

"The Xerox Corporation and Electronic Data Systems put the final touches on what is considered the largest commercial outsourcing contract ever awarded . . . Xerox confirmed yesterday that it would turn over all its worldwide computer and telecommunications networks for EDS to operate . . . The 10 year, $3.2 billion contract is not only the biggest such deal in the growing 'outsourcing' market, but also analysts said it was the first such agreement made on a global scale . . . 1700 Xerox information-system workers would transfer to EDS by the end of the year."

(New York Times, 15 June 1994)

Companies are increasingly turning to outsourcing of all kinds of support and management processes. Outsourcing by itself is not a holonic business system, but it is part of every holonic network. The mindset of outsourcing and the holonic business system are different.

Outsourcing—transferring selected functions or services and delegating day-to-day management responsibility to a third party supplier—is not a new idea. Its use, however, has expanded rapidly in the 1990s in response to the ideas embodied in Business Process Reengineering.

As companies undertake Business Process Reengineering efforts, they find that much management energy is spent in maintaining support and management processes that could better be maintained by companies for which they are the core business process. Tom Peters suggests that if a company cannot sell its services in a particular process on the open market it should consider finding a contractor who does just that, i.e. runs "unsalable" operations.

Outsourcing is not merely "contracting out." While contracting out is often of limited duration, outsourcing is a long-term commitment to another company delivering a service to your company or the holonic network.

While providers of contracted services sell them as products, providers of outsourcing tailor services to the customer's needs. While a company uses external resources when it contracts out, when it employs outsourcing it usually transfers its internal operations—including staff—to the supplier of outsourcing services.

While in a contracting relationship the risk is held by the customer and managed by the supplier, in an outsourcing relationship there is more equal sharing of risk. Greater trust is needed to engage successfully in an outsourcing arrangement than in a simple contracting situation. This is because in outsourcing the supplier also assumes the risk but the customer is more permanently affected by any failure by the supplier. While contracting is done within the model of a formal customer – supplier relationship, the model in an outsourcing relationship is one of true partnership.

ADVANTAGES AND CONCERNS

For the company that seeks to outsource functions or activities, the model provides many advantages. First are the simple cost issues. Fixed costs are avoided in that the company does not have to maintain the process through peak and slack periods. Second, there are often total cost savings in that the provider of outsourcing services can provide the services cheaper than the company can (if the company could do it, it would be selling the service on the open market, hence Peters's dictum).

In-house service processes are staffed to cope with crises and peak demand. As well, they often cover the landscape of skills, but are not deep in any one skill. An outsourced support process can be staffed to meet day-to-day needs, secure in the knowledge that there is adequate staff in reserve for peak loads, and adequate specialized staff to bring on board quickly and cost efficiently.

If the service-providing company is at the cutting edge, it is constantly reengineering its core processes to bring clients increased efficiency and cost effectiveness. It is able consistently to reduce the cost to clients in real terms.

Second are the service issues. Having an agreement with a provider of a particular service gives a company access to a wider skill base than it would have in-house. This access provides the company with more flexibility than it would have if it had to recruit or contract in specific skills for specialized work. The client can change the scope of service any time with adequate notice, not having to face the issues of "ramping up" or downsizing. Working with a company whose core business process is providing a particular service also improves the level of service to client companies above what they are often able to provide for themselves.

Third, creating a good outsourcing relationship allows the client company to maintain control over its needs and sets accountability firmly with the partnering service provider. The clear separation of roles between client and supplier ensures that service levels and associated costs can be properly identified and controlled to a degree rarely seen in-house. All of this can be done without the internal political issues that so often clutter relations between support and management process managers who are seen by their internal customers as merely service providers.

Finally, and most important, it allows the client company to focus its energies on its core business processes. It focuses on improving its competitive position and on searching the marketplace for opportunities in which to compete.

Of course, companies thinking about outsourcing some of their support processes have many concerns.

One set of concerns revolves around the loss of in-house expertise and the possible coinciding loss of competitiveness, and the loss of control over how the services will be provided.

A second set of concerns revolves around becoming locked in with one supplier, and the possibility of "supplier creep" or "hollowing" into other areas of the business. Along with this is the fear that a supplier, once it has solidified its position, might save its cutting-edge technology for new accounts while letting its old—locked in—accounts suffer with stagnant technology.

Both sets of fears and concerns reflect the basic reticence of business leaders to engage in long-term relationships based on the kind of trust and "partnership" necessary to function in a holonic network.

A third set of concerns revolves around the internal changes that will be necessary to effect the kind of business change that will occur when support and management processes are shed. The cost and logistics of planning and implementing changes to any process are considerable. But it must always be balanced against the opportunity of upgrading capability in another area.

It is important for a company to understand what is driving its need for outsourcing. Is it simply cost? Is it that management feels distracted by having to deal with many functions and activities it feels are ancillary to its true mission? Is it a strategic decision not to maintain a rapidly changing technology that, when closely examined, is associated with a process that can be deemed as a support or management process? This was the case we described in Chapter 2 when CTB took the decision not to pursue imaging technology.

OUTSOURCED SERVICES AND SERVICE PROVIDERS

Our idea is that, eventually, within any holon in the holonic network, all support and management processes will be outsourced. Frequently this will be to other nodes in the network.

Many processes have been outsourced in some businesses. The most likely candidates for outsourcing are computer and information services, and administrative services such as payroll, employee benefits and accounts payables or receivables. There are also opportunities in security, cafeteria, tax preparation and environmental compliance areas.

Providers of these services are coming from across the spectrum, from the traditional computer services giants such as EDS and the computer services arm of IBM, to the Big Six accounting and consulting firms, to other service groups within large companies.

For instance, in the UK, IBM Business Administration Services, has provided sales administration services, accounting services, order processing, invoicing and debt collection, and a host of other services—even customer complaint management—to IBM's sales force since the 1950s. In 1994 IBM Business Administration Services began marketing its services to other companies throughout Europe.

In the US, IBM is on the same path. In June 1994 IBM signed a three-year contract with the aerospace unit of AlliedSignal, Inc., for computer and network support services. Integrated Systems Solutions, the IBM computer services arm, said, it would provide a customer service center for training, technology support and asset management. A number of AlliedSignal employees were to transfer to Integrated Systems Solutions as part of the outsourcing arrangement.

In early 1994 IBM UK commissioned a study of the potential outsourcing market, which found that UK industry and government was outsourcing about $500 million in 1993, and that the potential market by 1997 was over $10 billion. The survey found that about 30 percent of this potential market is in process industries, 28 percent in retail businesses, 27 percent in government, and 15 percent in manufacturing of discrete goods. Of the potential market, 61 percent is with companies with over 1000 employees. With the arrival of holonic networks the survey seems to have underestimated the market potential, especially in the discrete manufacturing sector.

The study confirms not only the response Coopers & Lybrand has received to its marketing efforts in the outsourcing of accounting, internal audit and other areas, but also the increasing importance in the UK of the phenomenon known as "market testing."

In market testing, the national government is forcing civil servants to compete for their jobs against private sector providers of the same services. In May 1994 the magazine *Management Today* wrote:

"In pursuing the policy, the Government asks, with a chain of brutally simple logic, three questions of all aspects of its business: does this activity need to be done?—if not abolish it; could it be privatised?—if yes, do so; are there strategic reasons for contracting out?—again, if yes, do so. But if not, and only then, you go for the fourth and final solution—you market test it.

In 1992 and 1993, the Government, piggybacking on earlier efforts by local government to outsource activities from trash collection to tree trimming, market tested around two dozen departments, with a total cost of operations of about $890 million. They ranged in size from the tiny $2.9 million expenditure at Her Majesty's Treasury to $130 million of work at the Home Office. According to Cabinet Office figures, competitive tendering could save $203 million at a market testing cost of $28 million, for net savings of $175 million.

However, by mid-1994 only four departments had completed their transfer of operations to winning candidates. Much of the work put to market test was high value information technology.

Many states in the US have also been looking to have IT providers run some of their departmental resources, although the Federal government has not yet looked into such a possibility seriously; some would say this is shameful, given all the available opportunities. In the US, the movement to "reengineer government" has adherents in both the Republican and Democratic camps. Local governments have outsourced activities from trash collection in cities and towns around the country, to running public schools in Baltimore, and even to private police forces. On the federal level, a private company has built and managed detention centers for the Immigration and Naturalization Service, and private vendors run many services at national parks.

There are several downsides to market testing, UK critics say. For one, whether ultimately the civil servants maintain their jobs under their old employers or are transferred to the staff of the winning bidder—a common occurrence for staff of companies where outsourcing occurs—they go through months or even years of agony during the competitive tender process.

Another problem is that, when all is said and done, almost 70 percent of the work stays in-house, which leads many potential bidders to shy away—making it to the short list of three gives a company not a one-in-three chance of getting the contract, but less than a one-in-six chance since more than half the work stays home. Critics who would like to see even more savings argue that the sizes of the blocks of work put out to bid are small, and that they are in capital-intensive areas—computer services mostly—rather than in labor-intensive areas, where there could be larger savings.

But the strongest criticism is that the Government is seeking to outsource functions and not whole processes or services that touch the customer. As one consultant familiar with the effort and unsuccessful in one of the largest bids told *Management Today*, "when a department is looking at what it should market test, arguably it should be seeking to test the true services that are getting delivered. It is, after all, in delivering the services that you have the greatest opportunity to increase value—either for the benefit to the recipient or in reducing the cost."

That was not so with some earlier efforts in the 1980s, which sought to privatize some service functions, and out of which came a company that tried to carry outsourcing to a true holonic model. The company was called Service Interface, and its short life is instructive.

SERVICE INTERFACE

How a Holonic Network Came Into Being, and the Reasons for its Eventual Demise—A Danish Cleaning Company Sets a World Class Example

There is an old saying in the cleaning business: "It may be waste to you, but it is bread and butter to us."

The Danish company ISS makes the point as well as any other in the world, having grown from 1988 to 1993 by 103 percent in worldwide sales and by 198 percent in profit, to a point where it had about $2 billion in revenue in 1993. Since the late 1980s, the company has had an aggressive Total Quality program, a rarity in cleaning companies. This is despite the service sector as a whole being very active in total quality driven improvement.

Started in 1901 as a Danish-based security company, it diversified in 1934 into cleaning, then began expanding abroad, principally in the Scandinavian countries but also with some limited overseas investments in countries like Brazil.

By 1973 ISS was a pan-Scandinavian business with small, local interests, mostly in cleaning, in other European countries. Its "German" company had cleaning contracts around Hamburg, while its "British" company was really an office that serviced customers in and around Birmingham.

But since the late 1980s a change has taken place. While country managers remain leaders in their own territories—although less autonomous than in the past—the company now has a strong transnational culture in which training and development are used to enable the application of new management ideas.

Country managers meet the chief executive of ISS Europe, Waldemar Schmidt, twice a year to discuss their plans and results. These fit within a four year strategic plan that is updated every six months. What is being done differs significantly from country to country and place to place. In Berlin, for example, ISS only handles waste disposal. In Austria it collects hazardous and household waste. Activities in most countries are guided by opportunities that arise within normal business. The UK is no exception.

The Growth in Outsourcing Government Activities

In the UK throughout the 1980s, those in the service sector found themselves increasingly undertaking activities in their customers' companies. In one bank, the carpenters and handymen were employed by the contract cleaning and maintenance company to avoid having them work under bank employees' generous employment contracts. Bank managers loved this outsourcing of costs, and contractors were only too happy for the added business.

Successive Conservative Governments sought to mimic such private sector outsourcing schemes. Compulsory competitive tendering of services began under the Thatcher government in 1982, with the Ministry of Defence as the first national government department to experiment with the practice.

Later the public hospitals were required to put their cleaning, laundry and catering out to private sector bidding. Although the Government could not require them to do so, as the provider of funds it could make life difficult for hospitals that did not comply. Both hospital managers and service employees disliked the idea: managers because they thought they would lose control over the workforce and workers because they feared a lessening of their bargaining power and living standards if they went to work for a contract services company.

While the Ministry of Defence's contracting of services had been good business for service companies, the hospitals proved far less rewarding. Unskilled and semiskilled hospital workers went on strike and for a time hospital porters effectively determined who could be admitted to a hospital and who could be operated on.

A Vision of Bundled Services

In 1984 The Contract Cleaning and Maintenance Association (CCMA) was a trade group of British contract cleaning companies. Several of its member companies such as RCO Support Services Limited had won contracts for Ministry of Defence facilities. CCMA members were also instrumental in negotiating a solution to contracting out of cleaning and catering services in hospitals.

Soon other companies, such as ADT, the global security company, started businesses in the same area. The ADT business, called Mediclean, focused on contracting out services to hospitals. By 1989 Mediclean had annual revenues of more than $40 million. ISS bought Mediclean in 1989.

It became apparent to ISS through running Mediclean that there are really two types of in-house service groupings required to be contracted out, as seen in Figure 6.1.

One is technical services, which involves skill-intensive services such as IT, building management, mechanical and electrical maintenance, etc. The other group is more labor-intensive services such as food services (catering), janitorial services and cleaning, gardening and the like. Other services could be provided offsite, such as food preparation and storage, and waste management. It was clear that companies needed to think of bundling their services, instead of selling each separately.

Cleaning has become a non-threatening entry point into many businesses. For instance ISS Servisystem, which handles large cleaning contracts, added services when it won a contract for a large Sainsbury's supermarket warehouse that operates 364 days a year on three shifts. Cleaners became warehouse support operatives who open all of the shrink-wrap pallets on which product is delivered. They also clean the various areas of the warehouse weekly. Rather than merely working to contract

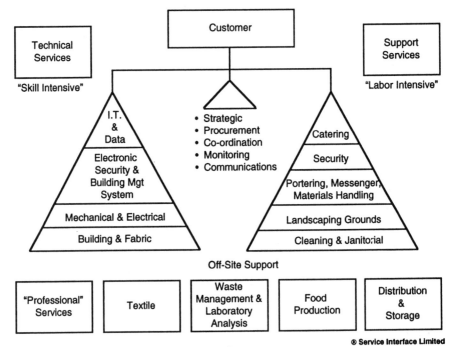

Figure 6.1 *Typical service groupings*

specifications—the old way of running a cleaning service—the on-site Servisystem manager has gone to Sainsbury's management seeking to increase the scope of services his people provide to include salvaging materials and damaged goods.

In 1991, Waldemar Schmidt at ISS was investigating the needs of the company's cleaning customers, with an eye to moving up-market into urban public transportation (bus and subway systems), airports and even semiconductor cleanrooms. However, at this time ISS was losing contracts and having its margins squeezed by the facilities management companies, which had increasingly come into large companies to consolidate services and manage subcontractors.

In order not to be squeezed by facilities management companies, which do not perform any services, service companies needed to band together into multi-service providers. After speaking with competitors, customers and people from other industries, ISS decided to try to form a holonic network of companies to provide a variety of services.

The ISS initiative was led by Michael Davis, who had been the CEO of Mediclean. He sought to form a network of leaders in their single-service markets. Along with ISS in cleaning he turned to Leigh Environmental, which specializes in waste removal and recycling; Sketchley, which does industrial laundering and janitoring; Pinkertons, the world's largest uniformed security company; Drake & Scull, providers of technical services such as mechanical and electrical engineering, as well as building managers; and Compass, the UK's largest food service company.

Davis, acting as the network's initiating integrator, brought together the CEOs of all the companies to discuss their various problems and how they might band together. First they thought about a trading company, but had difficulty devising an entity that would be suitable for all clients, sectors and services. They decided to form, in the first phase, a marketing consortium funded by subscription without employees of its own. Davis agreed to act as the consortium's manager.

A formal legal cooperation agreement was drafted—with care since the network had to anticipate anti-competition legislation (the equivalent of US antitrust laws). A shell company called Service Interface was established under the agreement, and the legal contract specified the operations of Service Interface for its first two years after start-up in September 1992. The member companies all acted as resource support nodes, detailing personnel to Service Interface at different times, and carried out their activities as operational nodes. Service Interface's board was made up of the CEOs of each of the five participating companies and a divisional MD of Compass.

Over the first months some member companies ran joint seminars for potential clients, while others formed project teams to look into issues that crossed their boundaries; for example, Leigh Environmental and ISS looked at developing waste management systems which separate at source the contaminated and toxic wastes from low cost waste, to allow the low cost, low risk waste to be sent to inexpensive landfills. Special interest groups were formed to look into opportunities in such markets as retail, aviation, health and pharmaceuticals.

As well, the member companies began looking within their own contracts to find areas where they could cross-sell services from one of the network partners. From such efforts, several virtual service companies were formed, tailoring level of service to particular customers. ISS held the contract for cleaning the Atomic Energy Authority at Harwell, and successfully persuaded

Harwell management to ask Leigh Environmental to help with waste management. In another instance, ISS supported Compass in its contracts to run British Telecom's food services across the country.

By 1993, rifts began to appear over competition between Compass and ISS. For most partners, hospitals were seen as an opportunity. Compass decided to set up a hospital catering service, which immediately began competing with the catering done by ISS's Mediclean group. ISS looked at a possible joint venture, but was not prepared to give up its hard won position in hospitals. ISS and Compass resolved the problem by agreeing that Compass would not try to form virtual companies for any contracts it won in the hospital sector. This limiting of opportunity obviously hurt all the holonic nodes and the network, as it violated the trust that is essential for its operation.

Service Interface had another issue it needed to resolve—was it a market educator or a selling organization for the network? Beyond that, customers were also asking themselves; how do I contract with a holonic network?

The holonic network also faced the practical problem of integrating the different skills and businesses in its virtual companies. Each virtual company needed a leader, a prime contractor who would be selected from within the network. Drake & Scull seemed the logical choice, since it came from a background that traditionally handled contractual agreements. The Managing Director also had great experience. However, there are vast cultural differences between contractual and service businesses, and although Drake & Scull was ready to take on the leadership of individual virtual companies, it was beyond its capability to be the network's sole integrator and to manage virtual companies comprised purely of service providers.

The inevitable happened in November 1993, when Drake & Scull won a contract which was to be managed by them and include four of the other nodes. A dispute immediately arose over contract terms, which were standard contract terms in the building industry but unacceptable to the cleaning and catering contractors. The Service Interface board of directors had foreseen such disputes, and had agreed to a dispute resolution mechanism.

But the disagreement boiled over so quickly—and at a time when many directors were out of the country—that the network could not even roll out its dispute mechanism.

TUPE, Transfer of Undertakings (Protection of Employment) Regulations 1981 the UK's legislation that covers employment security in a transfer of undertakings, became an issue. With deadlines for handover approaching fast it became critical to solve the dispute. But local management took fixed positions that exposed all of the cultural differences and weaknesses of the network. Compass and ISS refused to work under Drake & Scull's terms, which caused Drake & Scull to look for another caterer and to open negotiations with another cleaning company beside ISS.

Many managing directors were also being criticized inside their own companies for their work in the network. While they had received much single service business from the holonic network, it was unlikely that they could find an integrator for the various virtual companies to work. Drake & Scull felt let down by Compass. They believed that because it had been entrusted with the virtual company contract it had to solve the problems on its own. It refused to allow Michael Davis to intervene and insisted on opening the contract to third parties not in the network.

Eventually the contract terms were settled. Drake & Scull continued as the leader of the contract, and new cleaners and caterers were brought in. Only Pinkerton of the original holonic nodes continued.

At the next Service Interface board meeting it was agreed that no one should take the blame and that the fiasco was a learning experience for all. It was also agreed that Drake & Scull could not be the overall network integrator; the only problem was that no other company wanted to take that job. The board decided that for the second phase of the holonic network's operations it would set up an independent management arm. Service Interface itself would be the contract holder—and the network integrator, supplying continuity of management.

This, however, seemed unacceptable to Drake & Scull, which saw Service Interface as a potential competitor in the facilities management market. Over a series of meetings the board decided either to make Service Interface a successful trading company or to wind up operations. In mid 1994 the decision was made to cease operating. It became clear that trying to create a holonic network of single service companies had too many inherent problems.

Several lessons can be drawn from the attempt by a group of right-thinking businessmen to make a go of a holonic network. They all revolve around the issue of trust in one way or another, and around the precept that we laid out in the beginning of this book that a holonic network has to configure itself constantly, searching for the best value in any given process.

To do this—to seek out the best group of players for each individual engagement and to form a virtual company—there has to be more than one node able to fulfil the varying subprocesses. In other words, there needs to be competition among nodes to be the best value provider. Without competition the network is nothing more than a group of companies that package their services.

There is nothing wrong with a group of companies packaging their services, in the same way that different practice areas in large accounting and consulting firms are packaging their services to compete against the service arms of companies such as IBM that has packaged its services. Both look to work for companies that wish to outsource their support and management processes. Although there is nothing wrong with that model, it is not holonic. It is setting the stage for a holonic model.

Service Interface never reconfigured itself, it just rearranged the leadership role, and who would negotiate the contract with the customer. Service Interface never circulated the customer's requirements to seek bids from the network participants. This is a feature of holonic networks as they start virtual companies. The company that held the contract took the risk, whereas in a holonic network all of the participating holons share the risk.

Finally, there was really no sense of shared values, and no up-front agreement as to the "rules of the game," about what was to be expected from the integrator in any particular virtual company and what was to be expected of the other players.

There were three other subsidiary reasons why the enterprise failed. First, the charter was never fully defined. Was Service Interface a market educator or sales device? Second, the network tried to solve all its issues at the CEO level. We have repeatedly observed that it is the people who do the work who should work out the problems. Third, we know that leadership cannot reside in one entity only. Like each virtual company, which is organic, so too leadership must be organic. Each contract has a different emphasis and therefore requires a different skill at the lead.

FROM "OUTSOURCING" TO SUPPORT NODE WITHIN THE NETWORK

Outsourcing can be a valuable tool for an individual company to employ if it is trying to focus on core business processes, and reduce cost and waste in support processes. Taken to the holonic network, the idea can be extremely powerful.

Let us go back to the example of MEGA-PC discussed in Chapter 1. Support and management processes such as accounts payable and receivable, IT system management, accounting support, transportation, product maintenance, human resources and the like are common to all the nodes in the holonic network.

If each node continues to do these activities on its own, there is considerable redundancy of effort, and considerable cost. But if one node in the network does one or more of these activities for the others, the total cost is considerably reduced.

Take just the accounts payable and receivable. Assume that each of five manufacturing nodes maintains an accounts payable and receivable function, and also the associated activities of receiving, traffic department, parts planning and purchasing. For a typical manufacturing company the associated indirect costs can be as much as 15 percent.

Assume a typical ratio for these five nodes of 2.5:1 indirect to direct fully burdened labor cost, and that at each step the material content is 60 percent of the cost of goods sold (COGS). Spread over five manufacturing nodes, this could translate into as much as 10 percent of the final COGS.

A specialized support node, such as AMEX Purchasing Card Division working with FedEx can do the same activities for 2–3 percent of COGS, saving the network 7–8 percent. This saving could then be employed either for reduced costs to the virtual company's customer—more competitive bids if that customer is industrial or more competitive price if the customer is the final consumer—or as additional profit to be shared throughout the network.

There are a host of additional benefits beyond the simple cost savings. A service node that stretches across all of the nodes in a network binds each virtual company and the entire network together. The departure of a manufacturing node becomes a costly proposition, since it would have to re-incur the costs of the support and management processes when it "goes it alone."

Pressure to maintain core competencies would be increased for all nodes, since it is core competence that keeps each node in the holonic network. This pressure, in turn, assures a more competitive holonic network.

Communication within the holonic network is also simplified, since all nodes share the same support and management nodes, who are in turn motivated to higher performance for the good of the network and the increased profitability of each individual node through the network's growth.

As with every ideal, there are potential problems with expanding support and management nodes. They do have

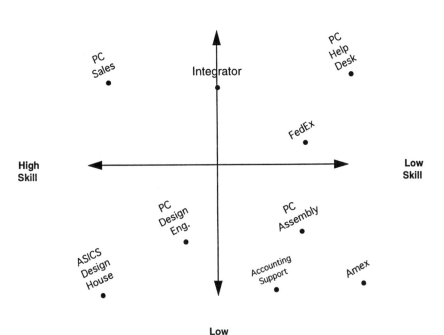

Figure 6.2 *Degree of people contact versus degree of specialized skills*

different ways of working, and integrating all of them into tight virtual companies can become problematic. Figure 6.2 plots the degree of people contact against the degree of specialized skills needed for the nodes within our fictitious MEGA-PC.

Nodes with high skill and high people contact may have difficulty identifying with nodes that have the opposite set of characteristics. For proof, look within most manufacturing entities.

The sales group often does not understand the complexities of manufacturing, while many on the shop floor do not understand the competitiveness of the marketplace. And accounting always has a "solution" for every operational problem.

When many companies try to forge a common understanding, the difficulties are compounded. Therefore it is imperative to define carefully the mission and purpose of the network as a whole, and of each virtual company as it is configured. Each node must, at one time or another, be forced to see the other nodes' needs and expectations.

SERVICE NODES THAT SUPPORT PRODUCTS

While most of our discussion is focused on the internal activities of companies that are candidates for outsourcing—or handing off to a dedicated support node within a virtual company—there is also the need for companies to think about the possibility of outsourcing the support and service of the products they make.

Although many companies are outsourcing these internal operations, they are more reticent to outsource functions or business processes that have a direct connection with the customer. However, if well done, outsourced product support and service can be totally transparent to the customer. For instance, in the US, if you call Sears for a repair of a home appliance, either under the original warranty or an extended service plan, you will often be served by an independent repair person working under contract to Sears.

Support for a product makes it easier to use or easier to get. For example, Union Pacific Bank has direct lines from some car dealerships that will allow for almost instantaneous car financing approval. This not only assures that the dealer can make the sale—the dealer is the bank's primary customer—but it presents a convenience to the car buyer, who does not have to spend additional time locating the financing from an independent institution.

General Electric "help lines" have proven that product support can be universally applied. GE maintains a support group that can advise any user of any GE consumer product on almost any question. The staff is trained in interpersonal skills, and is supported by an expert system that guides a support person through a series of questions and schematics to get the correct advice to the user.

Although when you think of product service you think of keeping a product going, the level of product service often enhances the product in the eye of the customer. Lexus repair centers both maintain the product and add value for the manufacturer and its dealerships.

When a customer needs to have his or her car repaired—or merely have routine maintenance—he or she makes an appointment. This is of itself unusual in an industry where most dealers work on the basis of "get it in early (meaning when the dealer's service department opens at 7:00 or 7:30 a.m.) and maybe you can have it in the early afternoon, if you really need it."

If a repair or maintenance is expected to take only a short while, the customer can use the "business center," equipped with telephones, fax machines and PCs, all of which are provided by the OEM. The additional service of the business center does more than just give the executive customer something to do, it strongly enhances the perception of quality the customer wants from a Lexus—and the feeling that owning a Lexus puts you in an elite group.

Sometimes the line blurs even further between service and support on the one hand and marketing on the other. Apple Computer provides training and materials for community college instructors in the use of computers. The college benefits by having more computers and better trained instructors; Apple benefits by having instructors who then teach using Apple equipment.

Apple itself presents a wonderful example of the potential and the pitfalls of life in a holonic world. Apple designs most of its own hardware and software—that is the company's core competence, and its core business processes revolve around design and marketing. The company outsources most of its manufacturing and has done pretty well in working with its hardware suppliers as partners. The company also outsources the production of user-friendly manuals, help lines, training for distributors in repair service, and customer training.

But the company failed to realize quickly the full potential of its core competencies, and how they could be leveraged. What would have happened had Apple agreed to license its software to IBM when the original discussion took place in the early 1980s? The world might never have heard of Bill Gates and Microsoft.

Extending this notion to the holonic network, it is clear that there is a natural opportunity for nodes to be found to provide customer support and product service for the virtual company's wares—or developed by splitting the best providers of service and support from its host company.

It is helpful to map the production and customer usage of the product made by the virtual company. As we wrote in our previous book, often the customer does not know what he wants. This is especially true in service and support. When the network maps product usage and customer needs, it will almost invariably discover some form of service that is not currently offered.

Offering that support or service can then provide the holonic network and the virtual company with a BreakPoint in the marketplace. It may be a matter of enhancing the competence of a service-providing unit within a node, then carving that unit off to become the product service and customer support node for the virtual company—and maybe even for all virtual companies that form within the holonic network. Or it may be that no service provider in the holonic network would be able to provide that level of support and service, in which case the core competence can be "invited into" the network from outside.

Because "service" and "support" are very much based on the perception of customers—and final consumers if you produce for an intermediate customer—it is important to obtain constant market feedback. This feedback can help reinforce the kind of behavior the marketplace equates with good support and service, and can help upgrade the core competence by upgrading the capabilities of all service and support personnel.

American Airlines has created a feedback mechanism for its employees, in "chits" given by the airline to its most frequent fliers. This is clearly the market image that American Airlines would like to maintain and reinforce its loyalty to the brand. The frequent flier can give these coupons, which say "you're someone special," to any employee who provides what the customer perceives to be exceptional service or support. The employee's behavior is reinforced, and other employees may affect the same behavior in the hope a customer will find them special as well. Employees like the immediate recognition and can redeem the coupons for awards once they have accumulated enough.

Although outsourcing is an imprecise analog for what goes on inside a holonic network, it illustrates the relationships that are forged in the holonic network. Outsourcing brings significant benefits to the holonic network. Outsourcing is as much part of the holonic business system as co-makership.

7
Ways of Working within the System

Life within the holonic network is as different for individuals as it is for companies that form nodes. As nodes come together in virtual companies, everyone, from the CEO to the service operator or shop-floor worker, is involved in talking across functional and node boundaries. Everyone thinks about ways to constantly improve the node, the virtual company and the holonic network. Each person is encouraged to speak to the customer of the virtual company.

Business Process Reengineering has changed the traditional way of working. Previously people in the "back office" or "works" were deliberately isolated from the customer. Business Process Reengineering focuses everyone's attention on the core business processes that serve customers, and this attitude is carried into the holonic business system as well.

Each person in a node asks himself or herself constantly: "How does my work add value to the customer?" These customers are not the fictitious internal customers so beloved by Total Quality enthusiasts, but real people who have needs and desires, and pay money to have them satisfied. To answer the question of how they add value, everyone in the node has to know the eventual customer of the product made by the virtual company.

One British business designs and manufactures optical scanners for pre-press imaging. These products comprise expensive, high precision optical equipment and high-speed image processing hardware and software. This is because they handle the large volumes of data generated by processing color pictures for printing.

The business set out to design a new scanning system. The design engineers knew that the highest precision would be obtained by a rotary scanner. In this technology the color image is attached to a drum and rotated past the scanning head. However, encouraged by their CEO, the new product development team decided to visit some pre-press shops to see how their equipment was being used. Their findings caused them to drop the rotary scanner and to absorb their existing development costs. They then relaunched the project using flatbed scanning technology. In this technology the image is stationary on a glass screen and the scanning head moves past the image.

This radical and costly change in direction was caused by the realization that in most pre-press houses the scanner was installed in a crowded corner of the office. Furthermore, it was generally operated by the office junior. He needed the simplest and most robust equipment. A small invisible loss in scanning precision was more than made up by the enhanced reliability that flatbed scanning offered.

Individuals working in a holonic network often move along the process, even between nodes. In one business that designs and manufactures light aircraft, the salesman is also the design engineer. Later he becomes the project manager, then the test pilot and finally the delivery pilot. That salesman has an intense personal and emotional interest in the success of the aircraft that he has sold.

This physical and emotional identification with the customer— along the core business process—is a hallmark of virtual companies, and of holonic networks. Individuals put their loyalty simultaneously into the holonic network, the node and most importantly into virtual companies. Such an allocation of loyalty is quite different from a traditional business model.

The other holons in a virtual company are quite possibly small businesses with different cultural styles or business units of larger competitors. While people still get a pay check from their home company or node, they get their satisfaction—and their recognition —from the way they act within the virtual company or companies their node is attached to.

Theoretically, any one node could be involved in, say, 10 different virtual companies for the sake of capacity utilization. It could also have its own business and customer base outside the holonic network.

It is difficult for an operational node to belong to more than one holonic network. This creates problems of trust between the nodes. It would also create conflicts of loyalty for the people working in the node. What most often happens is that if a business sees opportunities to work in many networks, it will split its workforce into numerous groups, with each group attaching itself to a different network as a node, even if the nodes do the same thing.

For instance, Nypro is a small holding company based in Clinton, MA. The company originally made plastic moldings, but now also assembles and distributes products that use such plastic moldings, e.g. hair-dryers. Some it manufactures for OEMs under brand names; others under private labels for department stores. Some it only manufactures; some it manufactures and packages; some it manufactures, packages and markets. The business consists of many small nodes. The basic operating approach of the company requires that if a node grows beyond $3 million in revenue it gets split apart. The nodes are self-managed and there are central support services such IT and human resources.

There are manufacturing nodes, packaging nodes, marketing nodes and other types of nodes. Some customers are large enough so that one node does nothing but manufacture, or package, for a single customer. The nodes form into virtual companies for specific orders for specific companies. When that order is finished they go on to team up with other nodes for different virtual companies.

Nypro refuses to hire an arbitrator to resolve disputes between nodes, preferring to allow them to compete with each other. From this competitive environment and its core competence in plastic molding Nypro has evolved a core competence in equipment design. The business is today able to sell retrofit quick change equipment to other plastic molders.

CONFIGURING THE VIRTUAL COMPANY

Within a very short time of the holonic network sensing a market stimulus—an opportunity—a virtual company will come into being. The configuration of the virtual company happens in "real time." The open-system architecture of much of modern information technology enables rapid communication, which in turn allows for this real-time configuration. As stated previously, the holonic business system is the first business system to need the power of today's information technology for its operation.

The need for rapid configuration of virtual companies means that information must flow horizontally across all the nodes in the holonic network. All potential participants in a virtual company have access to the same background information against which to make decisions. This information includes that available through the knowledge network described in Chapter 3. It includes information available in the public arena, such as commodity and share prices, and information specific to the particular opportunity.

Today, in many regions of Italy, small regional companies form holonic networks. Company directors are given a matter of hours, or a day at the most, to decide if they want to participate in a virtual company. Many of these networks have been operating for years, in industries such as clothing, jewellery, and even agriculture. Most lack the kind of sophisticated information systems we are talking about—decisions are made in real time through face-to-face or telephone conversations and the networks are built on long-time relationships.

The Starguest system, described in Chapter 2, is an attempt to enhance these "natural" networks that have so long existed in Italy, with a sophisticated information system. Starguest uses this information system to close the gap in distance, allowing potential participants who may be hundreds or thousands of miles away from each other—a British air carrier, a bus company in Milan and hotel elsewhere in Lombardy, for instance—only a short time to decide if they are "in or out" of the travel package and virtual company under configuration.

In other holonic networks it is not possible for a node to decide in hours or a day if it wants to participate fully in a virtual company. A quick reaction is second to technical competence. For example, in a second-tier automotive supplier, as the virtual company forms, even the component geometry is undefined. However, the node can decide quickly if it wants to be part of the design effort. Then it can make a final decision as to participation once the full scale of the commitment is clear.

The asset manager has a critical role to play in the configuration of virtual companies. This system holds, among its knowledge base, information on the capacity availability and capabilities of all the nodes in the holonic network. It can therefore suggest participants in each virtual company. Once the discussions between nodes and the integrator are complete, the asset manager confirms the feasibility of the virtual company's plan and reserves the capacity necessary for its execution.

Sikisui does this; after a house is designed, the expert system determines if there are any technical design flaws. Then the computer searches its data base of providers for each part, sees who has capacity, and who can manufacture and transport to the location. Then the computer sends the shop order electronically.

Whether there will be a formal offer and acceptance, or whether a potential participant is obliged to perform through a capacity reservation agreement, must be determined when the holonic network is formed. The failure to create agreed-upon "ways of working" can lead to a holonic network's implosion. This was seen in the Service Interface case study in Chapter 6, as one node tried to grab more of the potential opportunities, despite its technical and managerial inability to do the tasks.

GRIGGS: A HOLONIC NETWORK AND A "VIRTUAL SHOE"

The capability needed to configure virtual companies can take many years to develop. But once it has developed, it can become a core competence of a company or group. The R. Griggs Group, a Northamptonshire shoe maker, illustrates this.

The Griggs family has been involved in shoemaking since 1901. Since then, the company has grown from a two-man partnership to a multimillion dollar organization. The Group remains privately owned and has its head offices in the original premises in the village of Wollaston, Northamptonshire, in the southern part of Britain's Midlands. The location has been synonymous with shoe making since the seventeenth century.

Max Griggs and his son, Stephen, aged 32, are the fourth and fifth generation of the Griggs family to head the business, as Chairman and Managing Director respectively. The Group has around $120 million annual revenue, and employs 2500 people producing 190 000 pairs of Dr Martens each week.

The story of Griggs's success is a remarkable combination of foresight, good fortune and, above all, prudent determination. The family tradition began in 1901 when Benjamin Griggs and Septimus Jones opened a village boot making partnership in Wollaston. When the partnership split up in 1911, Benjamin and his son, Reginald, formed R. Griggs & Co., with considerable financial support and encouragement from Benjamin's mother and Reginald's grandmother, Jane Griggs.

But by the 1950s very little growth had taken place since the company was formed. The three Griggs brothers who were then running the business, William, Ray and Colin, found that they were facing tough competition from at least 12 other footwear manufacturers in the Wollaston area. Although the situation was eased by military sales to supply the Korean War and National Service, a serious threat to the whole industry soon arrived: GB Briton's "TUF" working boot, with a vulcanized rubber sole and a production method that allowed vastly higher output than traditional methods.

Bill Griggs's incisive reaction to this ominous development marked the start of the company success. With G.W. & R. Shelton, another local bootmaker, he persuaded all the other Wollaston companies to form The Wollaston Vulcanizing Co. This was established as a separate cooperative and equipped with new molding machinery to make vulcanized soles for all their members. This enabled the Wollaston companies to meet the "TUF" competition head-on.

Dr Martens shoes trace their origins back to wartime Munich, and the nearby town of Seeshaupt. There, Dr Klaus Maertens, a medical doctor, was convalescing from a skiing accident and decided to make a comfortable shoe to relieve the pain of walking. With a friend—Dr Herbert Funck, an engineer he had met while fighting for the affections of a young woman at university—he designed a shoe with an air-cushioned sole using old tires.

The sole was the special feature of the shoe. Whereas the soles of most traditional men's shoes are stitched on to the leather of the upper, Dr Maertens and Dr Funck devised a way of heat-sealing the sole to create a cavity, or air cushion. The result was so effective that within two years, Dr Maertens and Dr Funck had patented and developed the design commercially, and the air-cushioned shoes were sold all over Germany, chiefly as "comfort" shoes for elderly women with foot trouble.

By 1959, the new shoes—which had become known as "Dr Maertens" or Doc Maertens—were selling across Europe, and the two were particularly interested in finding a company to produce them in Britain. Dr Maertens was so impressed by the strategy behind Wollaston Vulcanizing that the German offered Griggs the UK rights in 1960.

Griggs anglicized the name to "Dr Martens," and called the brand "AirWair." The first pair of British Dr Martens rolled off the production line on 1 April 1960. Called the 1460 in deference to the date, the first pair of Dr Martens was the classic eight-eyelet boot, still a most popular style.

Early production problems were soon overcome, and by the mid-1960s Dr Martens, known as Doc Martens or DMs by many, had become an essential part of Britain's culture. They had been adopted by one of the great youth cults of the era, and no self-respecting skinhead was properly dressed without a pair of eight-eyelet Doc Martens "cherry-reds." However, the famous "bovver boots" were also being bought in their thousands by workmen and women, sold on their sheer practicality.

Dr Martens have remained at the centre of every trend—right through the punk rock and new romance of the 1970s to the designer footwear of the 1990s. Alexei Sayle and Pete Townsend wrote about them, and Ian Dury, Elvis Costello, The Clash, Sting, Tony Benn, King, Naomi Campbell and Madonna have all worn them.

Lenny Henry had a red-nosed pair custom-made for Comic Relief and Elton John's giant "cherry-reds," specially made for the film *Tommy*, are now on display at the Central Museum in Northampton. Dr Martens are also featured in the Victoria & Albert Museum's permanent exhibition on twentieth-century style and culture.

During the 1960s, a fourth generation of Griggs—Bill's son Max and Ray's son Peter—joined the company. Because of the success of the AirWair brand and the need to expand, the Group gradually took over both Wollaston Vulcanizing and all six remaining Wollaston companies: Septimus Rivett, Humphrey & Smart, George Denton, Bayes Brothers, Phillips Brothers and G.W. & R. Shelton. To cope with the expansion of its business over the years Griggs has taken advantage of its location in Northamptonshire, home to hundreds of small, closely linked shoe manufacturing companies. Each phase of expansion has bought a new, local acquisition. "We've simply talked to families in the next street," says Stephen Griggs.

Most of these subsidiaries still operate as separate, semiautonomous profit centers and now undertake contract production for other members of the Griggs Group, as well as producing and marketing their own products.

Today the companies in the Griggs Group have a wide range of core competencies, which they apply to the Group's core business process of manufacturing shoes. They include the production of high-quality leather soled welted footwear at Desborough Shoes, including Dr Martens—"Silver Cloud" and "Getta Grip" safety footwear; contract closing at G & P Closers for Group companies; insole production at GB Footwear; and laces manufacture for Group companies at Arthur Whittle.

Some companies in the Griggs Group have their core competencies in support processes, such as the maintenance of electrical equipment at Gemco, and compound and mold making at Wollaston Vulcanizing. Wollaston Vulcanizing also continues to make every Dr Martens sole produced in the world, and licenses other UK footwear manufacturers to produce their own footwear ranges using the Dr Martens sole.

Griggs has always been prepared to make significant investment in the best proven technology and equipment, from injection-molding machinery to production-line track systems that bring the work to the craftsman.

THE ROLE OF THE VIRTUAL COMPANY INTEGRATOR

The integrator of a virtual company is different from the initiator of a network. A network initiator is often a visionary who sees how putting pieces together will create a better core business process—the people within the governments and business communities of northern Italy who created the Starguest network, for instance. The virtual company integrator is more concerned with making sure the defined business process moves along, arbitrates disputes, manages contracts with customers, keeps tabs on performance measurement, etc.

In practice, there are two types of virtual companies, and therefore two types of virtual company integrator. In the first type, where a new product is being designed, the virtual company integrator is the "plugger and runner," finding players to participate in the process, deciding which of competing nodes presents the best value for the customer. In the second type, such as at Griggs, the complete network has been defined and is continuously servicing different prosumer requests, and the integrator is much more involved with customer and contract relations.

The way in which the integrator of the virtual company interacts with each type of virtual company is different but is based on the same ideas.

The integrator involved in the defining of a virtual company, its processes and products, is the more interesting example. This requires the integrator to match each node's capabilities and core competencies to the opportunity. This role is similar to a systems' integrator in the automation industry. But using holonic concepts, this integrator is able to produce an outcome that is far better for both the customer and the network.

In the old, classic scenario for a company that wants to purchase the automation to assemble its complex product, the company brings an automation system integrator into the design process early in the development life of the product. To bid competitively on this project, the systems' integrator uses prototypes or drawings of the new product as the base of the design.

However, the systems' integrator will bid a proposal with a lean margin, hoping to get the job. If he is successful, he negotiates a contract that typically locks in the performance requirements for the system such as throughput, rate per hour, uptime and quality along with a very compressed schedule. The contract negotiations typically also lower the price. Upon completion of the design, the systems' integrator will build the system, debug it and deliver it to the customer's manufacturing floor. There it will undergo an acceptance test, and if accepted the project is done.

The customer wins if there is a stable product design, where changes do not occur during the design-and-build phase of the project. But most customers do not have a stable design, and must go back to the automation house for changes. The systems' house wins in this case, because it charges dearly for the changes in order to improve its severely depleted margin.

Inevitably, the result is a loss of time for everyone, as all participants negotiate each design change and its cost, and everyone compromises in order to meet the design date (which usually is not made in any event). The customer gets the machine late, and has paid dearly for changes he considers necessary. The systems' house has upset his customer's expectations because of the time delay. Performance criteria may have been compromised in order to meet the—already late—delivery date.

In a holonic network the approach is to develop a relationship between the customer—truly a prosumer—and the automation house. Selection is based on capability and the ability to meet the customer's requirements, not on a confrontation and competitive bid—co-makership at its best. Once the selection has been made, a design team is pulled together to spend four to six weeks developing the conceptual design, with the cost shared by both parties.

The systems' house is paid for the conceptual design, so it can make money during the early phase of the order. The design team includes all elements that influence the automation: operators, maintenance and manufacturing engineers, and also the systems' house designers. The integrator may run the team during this first phase, until everyone trusts each other.

Business objectives are designed first, and a project schedule is developed that is updated every week. The economics, and criteria for selection of features, are also defined early. The process is defined, as are all the elements of variation of the process.

Quality systems are defined during this phase. For example, what would cause a bad part and how do you avoid it? Product- and process-cost models are developed to help make economic decisions. It is necessary to understand the cost of the process and the impact on yield and margin of the product and process.

Control concepts start with what information the people who will build the product or maintain the system will need. This includes such details as meeting the schedule, maintaining control of the process, and keeping them operational. In this way the operators help define the control system for the automation in the first few weeks. The owner-operator idea gets ownership on the floor, and improves operators' ability to work with the automation.

At the end of this phase, the usual result is a simplified automation concept. This has typically a 40–60 percent lower capital cost than a machine designed under the more traditional system. Because it is simpler, it takes 30–60 percent less time to build. The system is designed for multiple products (holonic flexibility) and not just the product that originally drove the design, because the economics usually require consideration for follow-on or complementary products. The system also has a higher uptime, because it is less complex and has had reliability as a primary design consideration.

The system also provides higher quality products because that was a design consideration. It is easier to run, because the operators and the maintenance people were able to be part of the initial design team. The systems' house has less risk, and therefore has a higher ability to make a profit and meet the acceptance criteria.

At the end of this effort, a contract is established to build the agreed system. The lack of confrontation has allowed each player to bring its expertise to bear on the business objectives, and everyone wins.

Within a virtual company, both the role of the initiator and the party who acts as the integrator may change over time as the output of the virtual company moves from design to production to market support and service. For example, in Starguest, the network was organized to increase tourism by creating high-value, customized vacation packages. The organization of each individual package is transparent to the customer. The government agency provided some financial and project management resources to move the idea from a concept to reality. Then it backed away, and the integrator role shifted to the other nodes in the network.

For each individual holiday package that is put together, the integrator is the travel agent or packager who receives an inquiry. His first task is to take the potential customer through a series of questions. These reveal the scope of the proposed package. The agent then searches the network for "players" who want to participate in the particular virtual company being created.

It does not matter which other role the integrator plays in the virtual company. However, it is critical that each virtual company has an integrator. The Service Interface example in Chapter 6 shows how critical the role is. It is essential that the integrator sees his role as an entrepreneur and not merely a planner. The entrepreneur will assume a program management role, developing and carrying out the broad direction, timing, tactics, rules of working and allocation of activities in the virtual company. The entrepreneurial style often requires the integrator to operate with very little data, i.e. by "gut feel."

The program management role is quite distinct from the project management role, which requires detailed timings, monitoring and control of activities. A project management role, however, is often necessary in a virtual company. When it is, the integrator should not undertake this role. The style needed to make a success of project management conflicts directly with the style needed in program management.

Just as with the issue of what the virtual company's ways of working will be, if it is not clear to all participants who the integrator is the virtual company is doomed to failure. It is the job of the virtual company's integrator to maintain strong communication between nodes so that the leaders can share their successes and difficulties.

The integrator's role is to negotiate with the holonic network's nodes to form a virtual company, and to close the business between the virtual company and the customer. The virtual company integrator is also the arbitrator of process costing and subsequent profit percentage distribution.

If the integrator is also a support node, then it is assumed that the other nodes in the virtual company will use its resources in the virtual company. So if, for example, the integrator is a venture capitalist, it will expect to provide the finance for the virtual company. Care must always be taken as the integrator begins the search for the virtual company participants that it is the "best" node to undertake the task of the provision of support and resources. It is always tempting for an integrator to seek to maximize the use of its resources at the expense of other nodes' resources.

If the integrator is an operations node, then it is vital that the person who is to lead the day-to-day operational activities acts as the integrator. This is because the details of the contractual specification between the virtual company and the customer must have the "ownership" of the leader and team whose task it is to execute the contract. In the Service Interface case we saw how trust and an understanding of the operational and contractual environment was critical to the formation of the virtual company to serve a hospital. This trust was missing and it put the entire network at risk.

We have observed some operational nodes, such as first-tier automotive suppliers, create positions resembling "vice president of sourcing" to manage the integration of virtual companies set up to provide OEMs with major systems.

Although there are tasks of physical management and administration of virtual companies within the purview of an integrator, the real job is that of facilitator of trust and referee. The integrator is the virtual company's champion within the network. It sets up the ways of working—the rules of the game—for the virtual company, and reinforces those rules over time. Establishing the correct balance between trust and control is a capability that develops over time. It is reinforced by participation in the network, it cannot be obtained through training, nor can it be outsourced. The network integrator acts as facilitator to understanding each node's needs, requirements and business perspective. In the Service Interface example, getting the IT people to understand the pest control expert's perspective, and vice versa, was essential.

In the US automobile industry it is clear who the integrator is: the first-tier supplier, who gains the prime contract from the OEM. In the three-day house, it is clear that Sikisui's computer, which acts as the asset manager, carries out most of the tasks of the integrator.

We cannot stress enough the importance of the integrator's asset management role. The integrator is the node that asks others to play in an offer-and-accept model, or the keeper of the IT asset manager in a repetitive demand-driven logistics environment.

The integrator, it must also be stressed, is also the communication manager. The communications management task concerns configuring the holonic network's communications system to suit the virtual company. The integrator will receive market feedback and ease communication across virtual company lines to other nodes, as well as up and down the virtual company's value chain.

Virtual companies will be managed—or will manage themselves if they operate to their highest potential—through a system of open and speedy communication. Maintaining the open lines of communication and taking to task any virtual company participants who do not share information is a critical role of the integrator.

Finally, the integrator sets, monitors and evaluates performance measures for the virtual company. These performance measures concern not only the economic achievements of the virtual company but also the humanistic goals set by the holonic network—within which the virtual company operates and by which the nodes and the network itself are measured.

MANAGING THE VIRTUAL COMPANY

The virtual company, we must stress, is managed primarily on a basis of trust and agreed ways of working. As we have seen in the example of Aprilia in Chapter 3, its transnational network for motorcycle design and manufacture requires the kind of trust that small northern Italian companies have as part of their business culture. Aprilia also shows how this trust can be extended to business partners operating in the more rigid business cultures of Canada and Germany.

Trust can be simply bilateral. United Airlines gave Boeing a commitment to work to develop the most flexible new aircraft shape for the 777, as we describe in Chapter 2. United wanted to be able to reconfigure planes in a matter of hours, not the weeks that it currently takes. Such a BreakPoint for Boeing is in both parties' interest, since a plane in a hanger is not generating revenue for United.

As well as the bilateral agreement United made a "unilateral commitment." Such unilateral commitments are a characteristic of successful virtual companies. United knew Boeing would develop the jet anyway, and that it would have to queue up to buy them. Having some new planes in the fleet of long-haul passenger jets would be a competitive advantage. United also knew that no manufacturing company would give it exclusive rights to such a plane. So United simply got from Boeing an agreement to receive the first products off the line, which would give it a leg up on the competition, trusting that Boeing would honor the commitment. United then offered unilaterally to apply its maintenance and overhaul expertise to the 777 development—in the short run it may have cost United many dollars, but in the end both parties will win.

IBM, on the other hand, did not have any trust in Microsoft when it funded the initial development of the DOS personal computer operating system. IBM thought it was working from a position of power, and assumed that it was buying exclusive rights to the system. What happened, of course, was that Microsoft sold DOS to the companies making IBM "clones."

IBM felt it had been shabbily treated by Microsoft. But what had really happened was that it had failed to agree to the ways of working in the partnership. Mutual trust between partners in a holonic network and in a virtual company—and some sense of unilateral commitment by each partner—is clearly a critical success factor.

Whereas in the old-fashioned business world of competition and closed systems, information equals power, in the open architecture of a holonic network and within each virtual company, information is synergy.

In Asea Brown Boveri, ABB's multi-domestic organization one computer-based system, ABACUS, is used to consolidate the monthly performance of the 5000 profit centers worldwide. The data is collected from the Zurich computer center by modem on a rigid dial-up basis days after each month end. The data collected can then be analyzed by business area, country, segment or company. In the rigid structures of ABB's predecessor company, BBC, such information was available only to the executives on the corporate staff. Today, it is made widely available in the business areas. But, more interestingly, it is the CEO Percy

Barnevik who is rumored to be the most adept at the use of the system!

Performance measurement information for the virtual company will be prepared by the integrator. The information will cover typically the core business process performance measures if the virtual company is doing a project type role. If the virtual company is supplying many different customers, as in the Starguest case, it will not be feasible to establish the performance data for each virtual company. This information will really only be feasible to compile and tabulate at the network level and at the node level. At the network level, measurement will be about having attained the network's goals. It will also be about cost, quality, time, service and innovation of all the virtual companies created to attain the goals. We discuss performance measurement at the node level later in this chapter.

In Chapter 5 we set out the way in which process costing is used to distribute the profits from the activities of the virtual companies. Process costing is the method by which the cost is determined. The cost is spread throughout all the nodes in a virtual company and the profit splits are decided on relative contribution.

MANAGING THE HOLONIC NODE

Unless it is absolutely impossible, a holonic node should have its own profit and loss (P&L) account within the company in which it sits. It should be a separate business unit. The creation of holonic nodes within large companies is the way in which they can become like small companies. It is also how large companies can go beyond Business Process Reengineering.

Nodes are run on the lean management model. Business unit leaders are chosen for their entrepreneurial qualities. They are executives who manage by "gut feel," by priority and by capacity and by improving capability.

It is not even certain that each node will have a formally appointed manager. In ABB's 5000 business units, many do not have their manager formally defined, but operate as a self-managing group. Koa, a Japanese holding company, has some interesting management approaches. Mr Koa describes himself as the first historical marketeer. He believes that "history does the marketing for him." Whatever was good in the past will be good now. The Koa Group is acquisitive, when it buys a company the first act is to strip out all management. From then on a group leader opens and closes the factory and the remaining management tasks are delegated to the process operators. At Nypro, units are split when they get too large to be self-managing.

The head of each node is a direction setter, one who is not afraid to change direction when business and market conditions dictate. The success of one node reflects on the others, and increases the core competencies of the entire holonic network. In a holonic node the leader must be a generalist and an information sponge and sorter. While this is not much different from most good leaders in today's companies, the reverse would be a disaster to the long-range effectiveness of the node. Somebody has to set the direction such as where to invest in new competencies. Someone also has to articulate the direction and provide the means for its achievement.

Growth for a node means developing new core competencies. It would be dangerous though for a company to assume that it can take every one of its current processes, core, management and support, and make them excellent. Thus, the leader of a node must choose which capabilities to concentrate on and which to outsource. Once excellence is achieved in core competencies, then backsourcing of capabilities can be undertaken to develop new core competencies. However, these new core competencies must be distanced from existing core competencies, as Koa and Nypro have done. Otherwise, there is a danger of creating an unfocused organization.

The leader of a node must be comfortable selling—and selling the node's core competencies rather than merely selling the product of the virtual company. He or she must be a strategic thinker, not a creator of strategies. If a company is to compete on core competencies, and to sell itself by its core competencies, then its leader must actively manage and develop those core competencies.

You may think that such qualities are typical of owners or top executives of businesses. But unfortunately, according to Coopers & Lybrand's 1994 Made in the UK survey, there are too few of these kinds of people around. The survey considered middle-market businesses in the UK, generally considered in the US and the UK as businesses with a revenue below $300 million. Figure 7.1 shows that the leaders of these businesses spend about two-thirds of their time on internal matters of administration, staffing and day-to-day firefighting. In contrast to the needs of nodes they only spend one-third of their time looking outwards, in strategy building and in new business development. Some executives spend time on strategic planning. There is no evidence that strategic thinking has yet touched most of the business leaders.

Just like physical assets, the "new" assets or capabilities depreciate over time—in a real sense and not just in the accounting sense. They must constantly be developed, enhanced, renewed and regenerated. It is the job of node leaders to develop, enhance, renew and regenerate the capabilities and "new" assets within their node.

A well-maintained holonic network is constantly improving its ability to add value for its customers. As a node joins ever more virtual companies it becomes highly specialized, lean and focused. This is the condition we call "Process Taylorism," after

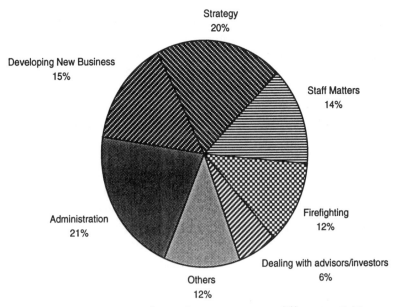

Figure 7.1 *Time spent by senior managers on different activities*

Frederick Winslow Taylor (1856–1915) who originated the ideas of time study.

Time study calls for a job under investigation to be broken down into several elements. Each element is then optimized by studying its cycle and reducing the work content to a minimum. A similar approach is followed by the node. The nodes within each virtual company perform a core business process that is seamless and held together by demand-driven logistics.

The leaders of each node also set the tone for the level of openness and trust, both within the node and across nodes. They are responsible for "relationship management" with suppliers and customers of the holonic network. This requires them to sell the holonic network's core competencies up and down stream. This is discussed in greater detail in Chapter 8.

In the thinned out, flattened organizations that exist in holonic networks, people are all close to the top. At Aprilia, the technical directors are as entrepreneurial as the company's president; they must be to make such an organization run. Throughout ABB, a group with over 200 000 people, there are only five levels from the shop floor to the chairman. There are three levels from the floor to the business unit head and two from the business unit head to the chairman.

Other organizations—especially retailers with a broad base of sales staff who have customer contact—think of themselves not so much as flat, but as inverted. The CEO of IKEA, which makes and sells upscale furniture, says he is at the bottom of the pyramid because he cannot possibly know as much about the business as those who deal with customers or suppliers.

Node leaders must strive to eliminate any trace of the "not invented here" syndrome, as this more than anything else creates mistrust. People must learn to piggyback on the core competencies of other nodes in the system, and the attitude needs to be "we can learn from them." As one CEO put it, "until we can prove otherwise, we assume the other guy does it better." This constant, if informal, benchmarking is a hallmark of successful nodes.

Along with the flattening of the organization and joint working with other nodes comes the need for employees to interact with both suppliers and customers. The Frito Lay route driver is just one example of such interaction. Frito Lay, the largest snack food company in the US, has no dedicated sales people and does not depend upon wholesalers or distributors to get products to the point of sale. Each of the 40 plus factories has a fleet of trucks that move goods from the factory directly to the supermarket or retailer. Each route driver is the salesman, billing clerk, credit issuer, and accounts receivable accountant. Not only is Frito Lay extremely profitable, since it has cut out the middleman's margin, but the company's cash flow has been the envy of the industry.

At the Providence and Worcester Railroad, a small freight-carrying line that runs through central Massachusetts and Rhode Island, if the train is running ahead of schedule, the engineer and the conductor will simply stop the train (it is the only one on the track) and make sales calls, visiting old customers or knocking on doors looking for new ones.

At Shell in Portugal, sales staff took on the task of providing technical assistance to their service station operators. This earned them wide respect from their customers. Shell management around the world began to wonder if their staff too could handle such a task.

At CTB, every member of every process team has some contact with customers or potential customers—after all, CTB considers it knows the process best.

But this does not work without training, cross-training and commitment from the top to give these nontraditional sales people real authority. And the way people work also has to change to fit these new roles. Employee empowerment needs the node's leader to have a vision and to express it often and clearly. Without this communication, strategic thinking becomes like a drunken man using a lamp-post—for support, not for illumination.

For instance, for three years in the early 1980s it was the fashion in the US to get tellers to sell banking products; some banks even set part of a teller's salary as commission-only. It simply did not work; tellers were not trained to sell, and the process of teller-based customer service was not changed in any way, so while an untrained teller was trying to sell a wary customer mutual fund shares, the people in line who simply wanted to cash a pay check at the end of a busy day were getting angry.

This kind of change in role and process is also complicated when there are unions and strict work rules involved.

The leader of the team in the node needs to apply the rules of good coaching and action-centered leadership, as originally set out by John Adair in his ideas for training the British army more than 30 years ago.

> "1 Set the task of the team, put it across with enthusiasm and remind people of it often.
> 2 Make leaders accountable for four–fifteen people; train them in leadership actions.
> 3 Plan the work, check its progress, design jobs and arrange work to encourage the commitment of individuals and the team.
> 4 Set individual targets after consulting; discuss progress with each person regularly, and appraise at least one a year.
> 5 Delegate decisions to individuals; if not consult those affected before you decide.
> 6 Communicate the importance of each person's job; support and explain decisions to help people apply them; brief team together monthly on progress, policy, people, and points for action.
> 7 Train and develop all staff, especially the young; practise equal opportunities; gain support for the rule sand procedures, set an example and 'have a go' at those who break them.
> 8 Where unions are recognised, encourage joining, attendance at meetings, standing for office and speaking up for what each person believes is in the interest of the organisation and all who work within it.
> 9 Serve people in the team and care for their wellbeing and safety; work alongside people; deal with grievances promptly; attend social functions.
> 10 Monitor action; learn from successes and mistakes; regularly walk round each person's place of work, observe, listen and praise."

In an atmosphere of openness, trust and self-managed teams, performance measurement can be tricky. Here, we agree with Tom Peters's thinking; when measuring the holonic node you need to look at the attainment of goals on a year-on-year basis, based on the objectives set out by the entire network. Just as you look at an individual's performance by asking: What skills has this person added to his or her repertoire? How has this person added to the company's value? You ask of the node: What competencies has this node honed so that it is "the best?" What has this node added to the network's value, especially in advancing core competence and technology?

A key to promoting the growth of the node is available to its leaders. This is the search for and application of new technology capabilities. Leaders must be aware that the progression of a new technology from invention to commercial success is slow and unpredictable, even when a technology has had its first commercial use.

Lawyers at Bell Labs were initially unwilling even to apply for a patent on the laser, believing it had no possible relevance to the telephone industry. Western Union, the telegraph company, turned down the chance to buy Alexander Graham Bell's 1876 telephone patent. Instead it offered to pay Bell to stay out of telegraphy, if it agreed to keep out of telephones. The inventor of the transistor, one of the twentieth century's most important inventions, believed it could only be used to make better hearing aids.

Commitment from the top is necessary to move any organization. It is also necessary for the leaders of a holon to recognize where creativity and innovation should sit within strategic thinking. Stimulating creativity out of context is unlikely to turn a poor business into a good one—it would simply make it do the wrong things better.

THE INDIVIDUAL IN THE HOLONIC NETWORK

We have already lived through a decade in which workers' lives have changed dramatically. Those who cannot work in teams, help to make decisions and then follow through on those decisions with actions, deal with information and machinery, and think ahead and improve their capabilities in anticipation of the next wave of technology and knowledge they will be asked to work with, are increasingly being left unemployed with little prospect of finding jobs that match their old positions in pay or stature.

Adding the notion of a holonic business system only means that the fluidity in corporate life will be increased, that people will now have to deal with crossing corporate boundaries and functional, departmental or divisional boundaries. People will need to be more flexible, more able to pick up the subtleties of different corporate cultures, as their assignment in a particular virtual company may be short.

Virtual companies do not have corporate structures or personnel offices. Individuals remain employed by the company within which their node resides. For instance, the group of engine manufacturing employees at Bombardier, a Canadian registered company, work on engines for motorcycles manufactured by Aprilia. These motorcycles are sold under the name of the German company that set the design specifications. They remain employees of Bombardier, whether they are working in Canada, Germany or Italy—for Aprilia or on loan to one of its suppliers.

Despite the name on the top of their pay checks, such people increasingly have their loyalty tied up in the holonic network, the virtual company and their node rather than in the corporate fortunes of their parent company. This is not just because their bonus is determined more by the network's success than by, say, the success of Bombardier's light-rail vehicle division, but because their heart and soul are being put—at the urging of the leadership of the node and virtual company—into their efforts to create the best motorcycle in racing today. To put it in Abraham Maslow's terms, their self-actualization increasingly comes from the performance of the network, the virtual company and their node.

As good team players, the Aprilia workers may be asked to move with the process between nodes; like the virtual teams in MEGA-PC described in Chapter 1. They may spend time in a node within the holonic network that does nothing but train, cross-train and develop people (indoctrinate would be too strong a word) for life within a high-powered virtual company.

Part of adding value to a person is achieved by training. This type of training, though, is radically different from the type traditionally given to operators. Besides TQM and Statistical Process Control training, there are also selling skills, listening and communication skills, management teamwork skills, and an introduction to management principles including accounting.

People who work in holonic networks have to be able to live in a constantly changing environment, with an ever-changing vision of their career path. They need to be constantly seeking to enhance their skill set, and the values they can add to any employer and virtual company. In short, they must learn to enjoy chaos.

BEN & JERRY CHANGE THE RULES OF WORK

Ben & Jerry is a Vermont company that is part corporation and part crusade. But you need not feel guilty about slurping down

Chunky Monkey or Heath Toffee Crunch, two of the company's many flavours, because as well as getting fat, you will be helping the planet while you do it. Ben Cohen and Jerry Greenfield, his partner, plough back 7.5 percent of their profits into the community. Ben says he "revels in the business equivalent of karma." This is the selling of goodness—Madison Avenue calls it "cause-related marketing."

They have appeared as guests on David Letterman and Joan Rivers. But Cohen and Greenfield do not advertise, they do not have to. They do good things and the media goes wild; they buy blueberries from Passamaquoddy Indians in Maine and nuts for Rainforest Crunch from rainforest tribes; they support family farmers, solar energy and the homeless; they protest against nuclear power-plants and bovine growth hormone; they saved the Newport Folk Festival from extinction, and their Harlem shop is staffed by ex-alcoholics from a local shelter. These are serious goody-goodies but that has not held back their corporate growth: their American sales for 1993 were $140 million.

Cohen and Greenfield met in high school in 1953 in Merrick, Long Island; "we were the slowest, chubbiest guys in seventh grade." Fifteen years later, after taking a correspondence course in ice-cream making from Penn State, they set up their first shop in Vermont. They have come a long away since then. In 1984 their Heath Toffee Crunch was voted the greatest ice-cream in America by the *Boston Globe*. Last year the company even opened a shop in Russia. Their company loves people to think up new flavours for production—Cherry Garcia was the brainchild of two deadheads in Maine—and offers free ice-cream for a year for successful suggestions. And its 500 employees love the company—the highest paid B & J executive is allowed to earn no more than seven times the salary of the lowest-paid worker (the average in the US is 70 times); two-thirds of middle management and half of the executive workforce are women and the company has an on-site childcare center.

Ben & Jerry's also has an interesting relationship with a company located near it but in a completely different industry. Both companies are seasonal to some degree—ice-cream production needs to be greater in the warmer seasons and the other company, Rhino, has a heavy winter season. Some Ben & Jerry employees spend the fall and early winter working at

Rhino. Rhino does not have to hire and fire seasonal workers and neither does Ben & Jerry.

In Maine, AT&T has a similar arrangement with L.L. Bean, a mail-order company that does its greatest volume just before the Christmas holiday. AT&T employees who work outdoors, such as line repair people, spend some of the winter picking and packing, answering telephones, and doing other work at L.L. Bean.

Those who are able to grasp onto life in an environment such as Ben & Jerry's, will have almost endless career opportunities. They will be offered broader exposure in more challenging projects along a wider spectrum of activities. There will increasingly be rank-and-role separation; a person may not be called a vice president, but he or she will be leading projects and teams that in a previous time would have been led by a vice president.

With self-dependency being the key, individuals will lose contact with their own core professional identity, even as they are adding to their individual capabilities. For that reason, it will be increasingly important for individuals to maintain ties with professional organizations that center on their area of specialization, be it electrical engineering or finance. When your self-actualization comes from the success of a dynamic performing node in a holonic network, it is invaluable to be able to stretch your professional understanding through external contacts.

In the first generation of holonic networks, larger companies are experimenting by creating small business units to operate as nodes. Smaller businesses are learning to join in holonic networks and virtual companies to challenge the larger companies. Individuals who can perform in the midst of this change will be the corporate leaders of tomorrow. In such a world, corporate leadership needs to show them that they will be allowed to experiment—and fail—without penalty. And the successes will be all the sweeter.

8
Marketing the System

Holonic networks do not simply appear. In many industries, there is a migration toward the holonic business system. Despite the new way of doing business, many old-fashioned activities still need to take place. One, of course, is selling. This is especially true in industries where there is a predefined hierarchy of value-chain players.

The best example is, perhaps, the automotive industry. While the European automotive industry has created a formal agreement with its supplier network, which we discussed in detail in Chapter 5, in the US the relationships between "The Big Three" and their suppliers are changing in a more freeform, dynamic way closely attuned to the creation of a holonic network.

Ford Motor Company and Chrysler Corporation are leading this change. While General Motors got much press attention throughout 1992 and 1993 for its efforts at browbeating its suppliers into more timely delivery and lower cost, Ford and Chrysler were "quietly" conducting a far more radical shift in relations between car makers and suppliers.

These two companies reengineered their new product design process so that first-tier suppliers of major components, such as seats and brakes, have become much more closely aligned with the design process.

The way the two companies have organized their design groups is different. Ford has created five design centers, each focusing on a different type of car: front-wheel drive, large car;

front-wheel drive, small car; rear-wheel drive, large car; light trucks; and heavy trucks. Chrysler has organized its design centers around major components such as front-wheel drive systems and chassis.

Despite the difference in design organization, both companies are setting up their relations with their first-tier suppliers in much the same way. In the old way of building a new car, or a new component for an updated model, the automotive OEMs created the design, drew the blueprints, then shipped those blueprints to the universe of "qualified" suppliers, asking them to bid on whichever subassemblies, assemblies and components they were qualified to make. Then the purchasing game started.

SELLING COMPETENCIES, NOT PRODUCTS

Under the new way of doing new product design, the OEMs designers create specifications for the new product—parameters of performance, size and cost—then choose two or three prequalified first-tier suppliers to create proposals and designs for the product. What does this approach mean for "selling?"

The first-tier suppliers are no longer selling a product that they make or can make. They are selling innovation and creativity, problem solving, and the capability to manufacture or create a network of subcontractors who can manufacture the components that will go into the product they design.

Let us look at how one first-tier supplier to the automotive industry has organized its selling effort to Ford. At Ford, within each design center there are "platforms," each of which represents a car model. Within each platform there are sections, which work on the design of each major system of the car, for example, emission systems for the Lincoln Town Car platform within the rear-wheel drive, large car design center.

Many supplier companies have become vertically integrated in a few core competencies. They have formed a matrix organization, with core competencies in system design and manufacturing. "Relationship managers" work at each design center, and at some platform levels. They have at their disposal systems engineers, who work with their engineering counterparts within Ford.

Most of the first-tier suppliers are large companies, with more than $1 billion in revenues, and have found and created core manufacturing competencies over time. These core competencies run the gamut from plastic molding to metal stamping to control systems. Most companies have 10 to 20 such core competencies, but rarely does one core competence generate more than $60 million in annual revenues.

In the early days of Ford's new methodology of partnering with systems-design suppliers, first-tier suppliers' strategies were usually to try to capture and manufacture the entire system for a new model. But over time the first-tier suppliers have come to realize that they do not possess all of the advanced technologies in all of the core competencies necessary to be the complete supplier of a system.

Thus, investment in core competencies—and the technologies to maintain them—has become a strategic issue. Companies must decide whether to continue to invest heavily in every core competence so that each is the state-of-the-art, or to invest selectively and be content to "maintain" their other capabilities. Here they realize that these may eventually wither, or that the maintained capability may eventually be used in the spares or after-market.

Some technologies, in all kinds of industries, are changing so rapidly that it may be impossible to keep up unless you decide that the process that uses the technology will be your only core competence. The imaging company, described in Chapter 2, CTB, does nothing but scanning.

Betting on the "right" business to be in for the future is a key challenge to today's executives engaging in strategic thinking. Making these decisions is even more difficult because the use of a particular technology today may not be the same as its use in the future—Western Union and Bell, for instance.

It is estimated that 40 percent of the cost of the car of the future will be in electronic components and assemblies. Until the early 1990s, most first-tier suppliers left the electronics solely to the electronics companies or to the OEMs electronics subsidiaries. If they continue to do so, they may end up being second-tier suppliers to the likes of IBM or Hewlett Packard.

STRATEGY BASED ON COMPETENCIES

There are a few options. One is to concentrate efforts on being "the absolute best" in a few core competencies and to become a subcontractor of parts made using those core competencies. This means letting other suppliers take the system-design work. They can either bid individually to perform manufacturing using the core competencies for each individual system that is contracted or, alternatively, they can partner another company that is stronger at system design and become a manufacturing node in several virtual companies in which other companies act as system designer and integrator.

A second option is to concentrate on system design, in which the company believes it has a core competence ahead of the competition, and can find long-term holonic partners. Then the company does not have to make the effort in time and financial resources to maintain its technology at the level of "the best."

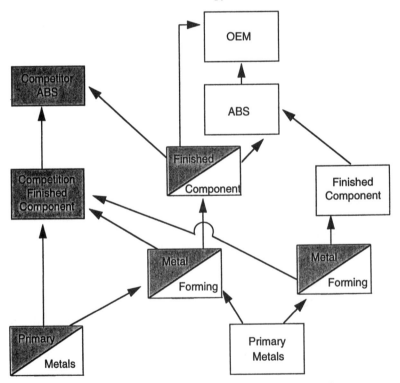

Figure 8.1 *Holonic network in an automotive supplier*

For instance, a company may have a core competence in large metal stamping, but believes the next generation of designs will require new casting technologies that may not be worth investing in.

A third option is to purchase core competence in subsidiary companies.

Figure 8.1 shows the internal holonic network that is coming together in a first-tier automotive supplier. The business units sell both into the company's designs for automotive OEMs, and into the designs of other first-tier suppliers. The initiator node has been buying core competence since the 1960s. It allows each business's management to remain independent and compete against one another.

In the early 1990s the company began rationalizing the business units, concentrating on the core competence each should maintain. What decision a business ultimately makes will decide the strategic direction it takes for many years to come.

This dilemma points very closely to the way "strategic thinking" has changed in the world with its new rules. In Chapter 3 we describe how strategic thinking is replacing strategic planning. Companies are less and less able to create strategies that say: we will compete in X markets with Y products sold through Z form of distribution. Companies are forced to create strategies more resembling: we will compete by X core competence, partnering with Y types of companies that have other core competencies to maximize market opportunities that most likely will come from Z direction, but may come from anywhere.

No longer does strategy mean putting a stake in the ground and responsiveness is bounded by it. In broader strategic thinking, how a company will compete is not predefined; the strategy—or the strategic thinking—is that the company will be a significant player in whatever markets can take advantage of its core competencies.

Strategic thinking is driven by what Hamel and Prahalad have called strategic intent. By way of example, Honeywell Controls Division has said that its strategic intent is to have the Honeywell name under every roof in the world. It does not say what control—a thermostat or an oil-heater kill switch—will be the component with the Honeywell name on it. Neither does it say what distribution mechanism is appropriate. But, every decision that Honeywell Controls makes revolves around that intent to have its name under every roof.

VP OF SOURCING: MOVING TOWARD HOLONICS

Sourcing has become an executive issue. It is no longer a make-or-buy decision left to an engineer. Increasingly, businesses are creating positions of senior vice president of sourcing to create a coherent set of protocols about what will be sourced and how. This vice president's main job is to determine what capabilities the company will maintain as core competencies and which ones it will shed. As well, the vice president works to select partners who have core competencies the company does not decide to maintain at the state-of-the-art.

One first-tier automotive supplier, for instance, currently outsources almost 25 percent of its cost of goods sold (COGS) to nodes that are their direct competitors to use their particular core competencies.

Intuitively, executives know that creating holonic partnerships is the best solution. But they are having difficulty replacing their old-fashioned notions of control and competitiveness. Creating a partnership based on trust and shared values is difficult. "We have always controlled our own destiny," said one first-tier automotive supplier executive. They worry most about giving a partner—who will probably be a competitor on other jobs—access to key intellectual property.

Ford and Chrysler have wrestled with these same issues over time. First, they have been through the sourcing issue and decided which core competencies to keep. As one automotive OEM executive said, "we have made a conscious decision to go brain dead" in certain capabilities. OEMs have even gone as far as to dismiss all of their engineering staff in that area as a show of good faith to first-tier suppliers that they would not be competing with in-house designs. These suppliers have thus come to the conclusion that the dangers inherent in others co-opting intellectual property are not nearly as large as the dangers in not being responsive to the marketplace. They have come to the conclusion that speed, flexibility and advanced technology are more important than control.

Over time the automotive OEMs have subsumed their desire for control to such a degree that top executives now readily share their strategic thinking with the top executives from the first-tier suppliers. This strategy sharing is an important part of the new executive bonding.

"Never have I seen so much selling being done at the top," said one first-tier supplier company president. Sharing one's strategic thinking and intent is the ultimate test of trust.

A Coopers & Lybrand study in the US found that chief executives whose companies were involved in alliances spend 23 percent of their time developing alliances, 19 percent drafting legal documents and only 8 percent of their time managing the partnerships. In a holonic network, we expect chief executives to spend no time on legal issues, and be able to transfer that 19 percent of their time to supporting the network. And, from what we have observed from CEOs of companies actively pursuing a strategy of intensive partnering, they are already spending more than 25 percent of their time working on developing alliances.

SELLING AT ALL LEVELS

While top executives of first-tier suppliers are hard at work selling to top executives of the auto manufacturers, the relationship managers and sales managers at the platform level are working with their counterparts at Ford and Chrysler to get an idea of the next group of projects to be bid for and assigned. They then work with their company's design teams to create enough background to become prequalified and be one of the select three who are finally asked to bid for the project.

These relationship managers work with Ford design center executives to develop trust over time. The managers constantly offer the services of their specialists to work with Ford to explore the "state-of-the-possible." They call on their own systems' specialists, who can suggest solutions to problems that have not yet been incorporated into the specifications. Getting the specifications written so that your company's thinking is considered enhances the chance of being asked to bid, and of having the bid accepted.

For instance, one supplier company has a core competence in tubular fabrication. A car chassis made using tubular fabrication would theoretically be stronger than one made in the traditional beam-and-sheet way. Having a chassis for a new model specified as having to be fabricated in a tubular manner would limit the number of potential bidders.

In this instance, bidders are asked to develop complete designs and prototypes for evaluation. Having a design bid chosen, means getting the right to manufacture and retain the ownership of the technology.

Once a specification is released, program managers or systems' specialists take over the selling. They spend their time acting as an integrator, creating a design and choosing second-tier suppliers—whether in-house factories or competitors—to create the highest value-added product. They spend much of their time working with the company's platform managers, and the OEM platform design teams.

Most of the communication that takes place in the building of a proposal and a virtual company is done by computer. Such information transfer capabilities are a prerequisite for being one of the prequalified suppliers asked to bid.

Unfortunately, the automotive industry is not fully holonic. Computer systems are still different at each of the OEMs. This requires each first-tier supplier to maintain three different systems.

The virtual company prepares its bid using a concept called target costing, which works on a simple formula:

$$\text{Market Price} = \text{Profit} + \text{Cost}$$

The assumption is that the market sets the price and management sets the profit goal. The only variable, therefore, is cost. Since the market exerts constant downward pressure on price, and management exerts constant upward pressure on profit, it makes sense that pressure will always be put on suppliers to reduce costs.

Target costing assumes that the virtual company has been through a process costing exercise, and so knows each node's process throughout the value chain and the associated costs. Each node's effort—and cost—must be "rolled up" to provide the final bid price. Such an exercise forces the search for additional value add that differentiates the virtual company's bid from others.

If a prototype meets the performance and cost criteria, the decision to source from a given supplier is based on the best value add. Value add to US automotive OEMs means the demonstration of the most innovations throughout the total process, including the aftermarket and subsequent recycling.

For example, a supplier company recently won a contract to supply accessories for a particular model. Under the previous system, an independent mail order company sends out a catalog a few days after a utility truck is purchased, and buyers can add accessories without any interaction with the OEM or the dealer. Under the system proposed by the supplier company, the dealer becomes a holon, and both the dealer and the OEM profit from the sale of accessories. The OEM does not need to order or stock the accessories.

The company has also simplified the procedure for buyers to get accessories, and tightened the value chain from the accessory manufacturer to the ultimate consumer.

If a first-tier company is not chosen to bid on the system design/integration job, then sales representatives from the individual factories or nodes are free to convince both the vice president of sourcing and the program manager at the various competitors who are bidding that their manufacturing facility has the core competence to be a second-tier supplier.

In this way a first-tier supplier can have as a linchpin of its strategic intent a Honeywell-like goal—to have "at least one component in every system in every car."

This is the very same strategic intent as that of Erie Bolt, now called EBC, which has redefined itself since being purchased in the late 1980s from a maker of nuts and bolts to a supplier of components that are produced by turning, thread milling, and a short list of other specific operations that the company believes are its core competencies.

Harry Brown took over EBC in 1987, in the middle of the recession in the Rust Belt. EBC had revenues of about $3 million, but was losing $100 000 a year. He knew something had to be done, but what?

One day Brown received a bid notification for a contract. EBC was capable of doing all the operations needed to fulfil the contract except one, for which it did not have the proper equipment. Loath to give up on any opportunity, he contacted a competitor that had the capability. They quickly clarified the purpose of their teaming—"profit," says Brown—and won the contract.

A short time later another opportunity presented itself with similar circumstances. Brown contacted another competitor, who learned from the first about the mutually beneficial and positive experience his company had working with EBC. Again, a contract was won.

From this one-off cooperation, Brown has created a network of 16 companies with diverse skills—from distribution to high technology plating to precision machining. Brown articulated his philosophy to Jessica Lipnack and Jeffrey Stamps for their book, *The Age of Network: Organizing Principles for the 21st Century* (1994), by telling a story of waking up in the middle of the night and figuring out what was different about EBC than any other company he had been associated with: "Most companies focus on the competition, how to beat the competition. We focus on the customer, how to meet the customer's needs." This may sound like the mantra of modern competition, but consider how many companies are still concerned about the idea of partnering with their competitors.

Although EBC still manufactures standard nuts and bolts in its own factory for sales through industrial distribution channels, its growth is coming from the business it garners through its network relationships.

When a bid request is received by any one network member, the first task is to decide whether the recipient can successfully complete the work alone. If so, the company bids solo, with no regrets and no hard feelings from network partners.

But if the request has operations the company that receives the bid cannot adapt to, a virtual company is assembled from nodes with the right capabilities. At any time there may be many virtual companies operating within the network, with each virtual company focused on a specific project for a single customer. Each node within the network may be working within several virtual companies.

Leadership of each virtual company is as organic as the network. The leader is the node that brings the most to meeting the customer's requirement—not always the node that received the bid notification in the first place. In other words, whichever node has the core competence that will add the most to the bid takes the lead.

Jessica Lipnack, who has described to us how EBC operates, calls Brown a "systems thinker," who has the ability to conceive of every operation not only within the network, but within the context of how the component will be used by the customer and the ultimate consumer.

In this manner, each node can optimize its contribution to the network and to the customer. We have called this the "synergy of value." Operating in this way, the holonic network consistently produces at 30 percent lower cost, and gives its customer better value.

EBC markets itself and the network as "the one source for outsourcing." To position EBC as a flexible supplier, Brown has cross-trained all of his operators on at least three pieces of equipment. For a $3 million company that was losing money, the financial cost of such cross-training was huge. But Brown believes the payback in flexibility and productivity was worth every penny.

The results of the network's efforts have been terrific. Every node has at least doubled its revenues in the five years of the network's existence. EBC has gone from 43 employees to over 100, with sales going to better than $8 million in 1993.

That may not be sufficient to make Wall Street sit up and take notice. But when one considers that *Fortune 500* manufacturers often have individual operating units not much larger than EBC, a compound annual growth rate of 54 percent would get much attention on the Street.

Brown is clearly the center of the network—the holonic network initiator—although every virtual company has a different integrator in its relationships with its customers. Brown drives EBC to set the tone concerning the culture of the holonic network. EBC gives access to its CAD system, its gauging equipment and even its engineers to any network member.

At one point, one member node started going after business on its own when the jobs were clearly better serviced by a virtual company. Brown, as the network leader, confronted the company's executive and said, "if you can't abide by the rules, then you should leave." The company left, and has lost revenue from that point on.

The holonic network gives power to Brown's credo: "ally, don't buy."

NEW PRODUCTS

EBC gets its ideas for new products by responding to its customer—or prosumer—needs through a bid document with specifications. This is only one of the six ways (outlined below) that networks and their nodes keep track of the marketplace and conceive potential new products:

1   *By being entrepreneurial.* There are a few individuals for whom the "aha phenomenon" is a regular occurrence. Whether they dream up the idea lying under an apple tree, or take an idea that was unacceptable to an employer, or see a fledgling operation that was not making it, these people define a product or service, identify the core competencies necessary to deliver the product or service, and find companies to participate in a virtual company.

2   *By looking at the natural evolution of products.* One product begets another, and so on. This works especially well for companies that focus on their core competencies. For instance, Norton Abrasives in Massachusetts started using aluminum oxide as an abrasive for grinding wheels and sandpaper. Then the company moved into using aluminum oxide in refractory products that use the same technology of forming aluminum oxide into shapes and then vitrifying them. From there, the company went on to petroleum cracking tower furniture (the little shapes that pack the tower where crude oil comes in one end and different grades of oil and gas come out the other. Then on to using aluminum oxide as propants to extend the useful life of oil wells, and so on.

   3M, by focusing on its core competence of "putting goop on a substrate," has come up with hundreds of products.

3 *Database investigators.* It is estimated that 90 percent of all consumer data collected is not used. Until now, there was just too much data to be effectively used by any but the most powerful computers. But with "massively parallel supercomputers," it is possible to digest and manipulate billions of bits of data in a short time. Thinking Machines Company, which manufactures these supercomputers, has also developed application software called—appropriately enough—Darwin, which takes consumer data and massages it to establish trends in buying habits that consumers do not even know are evolving.

4 *Market segmentation.* This old standby may be beneficial to holonic networks with their many virtual companies. In profitable segments, the network can compete on price and retain high margins, since its total costs are lower. In underserved segments, the combination of product, service and support designed for that segment will realize easier profits since the network is highly effective at efficiently meeting customers' needs.

5 *Customer specific.* There are several instances where a virtual company within the network concentrates on one customer. Intel has a node that works only for IBM. A Japanese oven company has an engineer at each customer location. Major auditing firms often have full-time auditors at major customers. Often, the node knows as much or more about a major customer's upcoming requirements than the customer does, and can tailor products or services to those requirements.

6 *Finally, there are prosumer requests.* For example, the one-off bids that EBC responds to, or the bids first-tier auto suppliers respond to. As prosumers ask for options or services that are not available using current technology, or are not within the holonic network's core competence, a data base can track them and, when enough such requests have been made, the network can seek to add a new product or service. Fine hotels keep such lists, and have over time added services such as fitness rooms, child-care services, and a host of others, as enough customers think they are important.

With the approach of holonic networks that seek to respond quickly, efficiently and effectively to prosumers, we are moving toward a time when a critical mass of one will be all that is necessary for a virtual company to add a new product or service to its roster of those it carries. We are moving toward the world of mass customization.

9
Going Forward

The progress of Business Process Reengineering is following a predictable pattern. First, the business school academics and management gurus came up with an innovation that they declared would confer competitive advantage, multiply profitability, improve flexibility and the like. Management experts took up these first ideas and spread them in all directions. After a while the critics moved in to expose the overstatements and to challenge the wilder fantasies. It is now possible to distinguish the elements of lasting value through the smokescreen of misinformation and mystery.

Managers who are practicing Business Process Reengineering have seen how hard it is to step back and challenge the very companies and functions in which they work. Instead of learning from past mistakes and triumphs a very few have managed to abandon temporarily every idea, principle and assumption and set up a new beginning for their business.

Throughout our previous book (Johansson et al., 1993), we made the point that it is possible to realize radical improvements in operational performance. This is achieved by step changes in the parameters of quality, cost, service and cycle time which characterize the processes of every business. We apply a variety of tools and techniques which focus on the business as a set of related customer-orientated core business processes. This is as opposed to a set of organizational functions or divisions.

In this book we recognize that core business processes extend far beyond the boundaries of the single business. Furthermore they offer the opportunity to serve customers in totally new ways. In Japan we have described how today it is possible to visit a local builder and design a purpose-built house from the catalog of many suppliers. They build the house to the chosen design and it is available for occupation within weeks.

This new style of customers, called "prosumers," require in their turn new core competencies from the core business processes. Each new demand requires new types of core business processes.

The analysis of processes has advanced from the status that is presented in most Business Process Reengineering approaches. The supporters of Business Process Reengineering methodologies have explained with some pride that they analyze processes to optimize customer value which is expressed as cost, service, quality and cycle time. This book explains that quality, service and cycle times are necessary conditions for competition. It shows that for advanced businesses cost has become again the most important factor for satisfying the consumer and the shareholder.

We describe how Starguest configures travel packages for each customer. Here the travel agent acts as an entry into a group of companies who offer everything from travel, to hotels, to sports facilities and restaurants. Those who buy a package take the quality, service and reliability of the process for granted. Price takes the most important place in making a decision.

In our previous book (Johansson *et al.*, 1993), we described how businesses must seek out and even stockpile BreakPoints. This retains competitive advantage in their core business processes.

Global competition renders antitrust laws arcane and forces the realization that there is strength in numbers. Those companies whose operating strategy is teaming with equally creative and expert technologists will win the global battles. We can no longer think of organizations, save perhaps governments, who will not benefit both in growth and effectiveness from the "synergy of value."

This book explains that in the new competitive environment, core business processes should be reengineered according to sets of rules. These rules are set for the interaction between firms and potentially for each customer order. A BreakPoint for each customer not each market!

Prosumerism and the demand for mass customization have become more than just business buzz words. Customers are demanding that they are treated as though they are the most important people. They want their requests treated as the driver of innovation in product, service and support.

The excellence of each business in creating BreakPoints and undertaking core Business Processes Reengineering is taken for granted. In addition each business must undergo a program of continuous improvement if it is to remain a viable participant in the rapidly changing networks.

The focus on core business processes in Business Process Reengineering placed new demands on the support and management processes—in particular on the "new" assets needed to keep them in efficient operation. In the previous book we dedicated a whole chapter to considering how to treat these "new" assets. Here we discuss how core business processes are configured for each customer order from a network of businesses. Each business is selected for its excellence in one or more processes. In this way "new" assets and core competencies are resourced not outsourced and relationships become cooperative rather than adversarial.

The experience of Griggs in creating a group of small businesses to supply its widespread sales operations is a good example of this approach to networking. The experience for many small businesses involved is positive in that it enables them to participate in a large business without the adverse social consequences that this often implies. For large businesses, the effect on flexibility of supply, quality and service and consequently on their costs and inventory is considerable.

In the Aprilia motorcycle manufacturing example and the others mentioned previously it is clear that Beyond Business Process Reengineering is concerned with configuring several companies, each with a particular core competence, into virtual companies. In each case the virtual company is more powerful than the participating members alone. This cooperative way of working has led us to make an analogy with holonic bodies in nature such as the Portuguese man-of-war.

Holonic biological organisms are entities organized in a multi-layer structure where each level consists of subsystems, holons or nodes. In the man-of-war the individual holons act together to provide a capability not achievable on their own. For example to trap, kill and eat a fish.

A holonic network in business is a set of companies that act organically. It constantly configures itself as a 'best value chain' to manage each business opportunity the customer presents. Each configuration of process capabilities is a virtual company within the holonic network.

What we have described in this book is hardly fanciful. To be sure, there are but a few fully blown holonic networks in operation today. There are hundreds of companies that are developing elements of the holonic business system. Others are behaving in a way that puts them on a path to holonic networks.

If your company is not already using some ideas in this book, you need to take a serious look at how you can change it. We firmly believe that holonic capabilities are essential for companies that are going to grow and prosper in the twenty-first century.

The cost of innovation is increasingly becoming too much for most companies to bear, especially the cost of the technology necessary to support core business processes. That technology is not only costly, but it is rapidly changing. For example, ASIC performance is expected to quadruple every two years. A further expense occurs in "ramping up" personnel skills and facilities to house, maintain and operate the technology. Information technology has come of age. Those who do not take advantage of the benefits risk becoming obsolete in a comparative nanosecond.

Only by rationalizing support and management processes, by investing in the technology necessary to maintain those that are truly core business processes and by finding partners to take over the other processes will businesses keep their core competencies state-of-the-art.

The holonic network has several characteristics which distinguish it from traditional business networks and partnerships. It is not organized hierarchically but has a shared value system with each holon capable of exhibiting the characteristics of the whole network. It is a self-regulating network which is in dynamic equilibrium with its market. Therefore the holonic network evolves continually due to its interaction with the environment and is self-learning. Access and exchange of information can be freely accomplished both from inside and

Table 9.1 *Qualities and operating styles*

	Japan	North America	Western Europe
Physical structure (geographic proximity)	+	+/−	+ +
Business structure	+	+	+
Entrepreneurial capability	−	+	+ +
Management capability (incl. info. mgt.)	+	+ +	+/−

outside the network. The styles of business operations vary by nationality.

MAJOR AREAS OF HOLONIC OPERATIONS

Table 9.1 shows some qualities and operating styles displayed in the three major areas of holonic operations in the industrialized countries: Japan, North America (as signified mainly by the United States) and Western Europe (as signified most closely by Italy, Germany and Switzerland).

By looking at Table 9.1, it is clear that all three areas bring particular advantages to holonic networks. Yet no one area has all of the internal qualities and operating styles that make it naturally able to support fully formed holonic networks:

1 *Japan*. The Japanese have well-developed networks of companies. There is good geographic proximity, and a business structure that is conducive to networking. The Japanese have highly formed management capabilities, including a good grasp of information management.

   But the mother company in Japan often appoints the managers of small businesses. They therefore tend not to be "self-starters" and have little in the way of entrepreneurial spirit. What is lacking in the Japanese model is an innate sense of entrepreneurship.

   It is a mistake to think of the founders and major leaders of the powerful Japanese postwar federations such as the Keidanren, the Nikkeiren, the Keizai Doyukai and the Japan Chamber of Commerce as entrepreneurs, or as representing entrepreneurs.

The Keidanren is the federation of leading industrial organizations such as the automobile manufacturers' association, the shipbuilders' association, the iron and steel federation, the petroleum association and the chemical industry association, with trading companies, wholesale businesses, banks, insurance companies and securities companies. The Nikkeiren is the Japan Federation of Employers' Associations. The Keizai Doyukai is the committee for economic development—the forum in which elite members can help formulate business policies.

In the early 1990s the zaikaijin, business elders, form a gerontocracy at the top of an ever more bureaucratic business world. As chairmen of their respective companies they continue to wield tremendous power, greater even than that of the presidents. The chairmanship leaves them with time and opportunity to participate in committee work. They enhance the reputation of their companies as they pontificate on what is desirable for society and add their contributions to the ubiquitous platitudes regarding Japan's tasks and future role in the world.

Business practice is to use outsourcing regularly. However, the supplier-to-customer relationships created in this way are rigid and based on a fixed pattern. This is a problem for Japanese companies that seek to work in a holonic network.

2 *North America.* One of North America's greatest social qualities is its geographic vastness and the feeling of freedom and opportunity. That quality that it gives its people is also its greatest drawback in creating holonic networks. The best North American companies compensate though, especially through innovative use of information technology.

American management capabilities are probably the most highly regarded in the world, and there is a natural spirit of adventure and entrepreneurship in the American business ethic. Although this spirit in no way makes American companies automatically inclined to be holonic, they are better positioned for success.

3 *Europe.* In Europe there is a high level of entrepreneurship and geographic proximity, which is even more developed than in Japan. These qualities make the European area of Italy, Germany and Switzerland ideal for natural holonic networks.

Holonic networks already exist in the regional groups in Italy, especially in the north. Here, small, entrepreneurial companies band together to form networks.

However, the Europeans who excel in this kind of operation lack highly developed management capabilities. There is also a lack of vision on a broad scale. Information technology has proved difficult to apply across national boundaries and old fashioned, relationship oriented, business practices could cost Europe dearly as the holonic business system becomes a global reality.

None of the shortcomings identified is insurmountable. As the idea of the holonic network becomes more global and the virtues of a more worldly outlook become apparent, European business leaders will use their natural entrepreneurial skills to adapt.

It is only a matter of time before American companies harness the full power of information technology to overcome geographic distance through communications. A great leap forward was made by E.D.I. Banx in April of 1994 with the inauguration of a system operated by a consortium of 13 US banks. The system not only allows corporate payments to be made via electronic data interchange (EDI), but also transmits remittance records.

Wire fund transfers from customer to supplier are common. Yet paper remittance records containing such information as invoice numbers, discounts and nonpayment for damaged or missing goods continue to be sent by mail, and processed by hand. The banks, and Chicago Clearing, the company that will operate E.D.I. Banx for the banking consortium, hope to eliminate 30 percent or more of the cost. This reduction in the cost of processing remittance records will pass to each client who purchases the service.

The Japanese already have a finely tuned decision-making system. This compensates for the natural lack of an entrepreneurial spirit in the personal style of most Japanese. The Japanese have taken what we call "horizontal and strategic" consistency to a high level. In many ways horizontal and strategic consistency is the key to twenty-first century strategic decision making.

Horizontal and strategic consistency assumes that a producer must first meet the current process standards. These are set in areas such as quality, delivery reliability, cycle time, service and product characteristics. Achieving these process standards is the "price of admission" to compete in the manufacturing world on the cusp of the twenty-first century. The horizontal part of consistency is then the short-term goal to reduce purchased material costs, and to reduce manufacturing cost.

While meeting process standards, company leaders look strategically at the future. This means creating scenarios and doing scenario planning to decide what core competencies the business must develop to compete 10 years or more in the future. The scenarios are developed without regard to the current product and service range. Rather, core competencies are the strategic part of the horizontal and strategic consistency.

Leaders need to take their businesses ahead of prosumerism and the process–cost curve. The only way to do this is to admit that you cannot do it all and do only what you do best. This means teaming up with those who do other things better. To do this, leaders need to suppress their ego. They have to allow their corporate culture to fit into the culture of the holonic network, while at the same time they must drive their own business to the limit of its core competencies. This means identifying and reengineering their core business processes to be truly the best providers of value for the network.

This is easier said than done. Lipnack and Stamps have studied teams and networks extensively. They have identified some pitfalls for businesses when forming virtual companies and holonic networks. In this book we have added a few from our experience:

- Undue reliance on one central company, resulting in an unhealthy co-dependency. The creation of many virtual companies within the holonic network reduces the chance of this occurring.
- Becoming totally dependent on each other for success—a special problem for small companies that may be tempted to "put all their eggs in the holonic basket." All of the success stories we have encountered—and all those we cite in this book—involve companies that have clearly defined when they will be holonic and when they will produce their own products.

- Pressure resulting from excessive coordination. If each company has a core competence, a clear understanding of its strategic intent and mutual trust and respect for all of its holonic partners, there should be no need for "excessive coordination."
- Lack of nimbleness, lack of response to market changes and excessive and over-detailed planning. Virtual companies have to work by feel—almost like a safecracker, holding the nob of a safe and "feeling" with his fingertips as the tumblers fall into place.
- Exclusive arrangements between entities that stop product improvement or response to the market. Holonic networks need to be as open as possible, allowing any node that can provide the best value for a piece of the process to displace even a longtime network participant.
- Failure to support a struggling entity, and the opposite, failure to replace an entity that no longer can participate.
- Failure to outsource support and management processes.
- Ignoring the ways of working within a holonic network.
- Overlooking the need for trust.
- Neglecting core competencies and the realization that it takes much focused work to achieve the benefits from the network.

As to the last point, one of us recently presented a seminar on the topic of Business Process Reengineering. After the presentation a member of the audience corralled the speaker in the hallway. He was employed by a large US corporation, one that is currently undergoing considerable difficulty because of its monolithic structure. Poking his finger into the speaker's chest he announced in all seriousness, "We tried MRP; it didn't work. We tried JIT; it didn't work. We tried Business Process Reengineering; it didn't work. We are waiting for artificial intelligence." Clearly he is not a candidate for a holonic network!

We close with approximately the same admonition with which we closed our previous Business Process Reengineering book. Finding core business processes and nurturing them through the application of Business Process Reengineering is not easy. Sharing and synergizing them with other partners is harder still.

It is vitally important if Western companies are to continue to grow in an increasingly competitive global world.

Automotive suppliers, building contractors and office services businesses join with such as Starguest and Griggs as examples of the way that many businesses have now constructed highly profitable and successful business networks which have gone *Beyond Business Process Reengineering: towards the holonic enterprise.*

References

Collins, T. and Doorley, T. (1991). *Teaming up for the 90's: A Guide to International Joint Ventures and Strategic Alliances*. Homewood: Business One Irwin.

Hayes, R. and Wheelwright, S. (1984). *Restoring Our Competitive Edge: Competing through Manufacturing*. John Wiley & Sons, Inc.

Johansson, H. J., McHugh, P., Pendlebury, A. J. and Wheeler III, W. A. (1993). *Business Process Reengineering: Breakpoint Strategies for Market Domiance*. Chichester: John Wiley.

Lipnack, J. and Stamps, J. (1994). *The Age of Network: Organizing Principles for the 21st Century*. Omneo.

Merli, G. (1991). *Co-makership*. Productivity Press, Inc.

Mintzberg, H. (1994). *The Rise and Fall of Strategic Planning*. Prentice Hall.

Normann, R. and Ramírez, R. (1994). *Designing Interactive Strategy: Value Chain to Value Constellation*. Chichester: John Wiley.

Stacey, R. D. (1992). *Managing Chaos*. London: Kogan Page.

Thompson, J. D. (1967). *Organizations in Action*. McGraw-Hill.

Index

Note: Page references in *italics* refer to Figures; those in **bold** refer to Tables

Index compiled by Annette Musker